Eucalyptus Globulus.

FOREST CULTURE

AND

Eucalyptus Trees.

BY

ELLWOOD COOPER.

The only Complete and Reliable Work on the Eucalypti
Published in the United States.

SAN FRANCISCO:
Cubery & Company, Steam Book and Ornamental Job Printers,
No. 414 Market Street, below Sansome.
1876.

CONTENTS.

INTRODUCTION.

In presenting to the public a printed copy of my "*Lecture on Forest Planting and Australian Gum-Trees*," delivered before the Santa Barbara College Association, for the benefit of the library, it is necessary to preface the lecture by the statement that it appears in print in consequence of repeated demands for the publication from several localities in the southern part of California. Forest protection, the want of trees, in almost every part of the State, is manifest to all owners of land, who are eager to begin the planting; the only question being—What shall we plant? The rapidity of growth of the Blue Gum, and the facility with which it can be propagated, is a feature of great importance; but information is wanted. Much that has been written on the subject is mere speculative theories, often contradictory, and too uncertain to merit the confidence necessary to base such an important industry. This industry not only necessitates that the protection should be cheaply and quickly obtained, but that the tree should have a value for mechanical or other purposes. This value gives confidence to the planter, without which it can not be expected the work will go on. The inquiry comes, What is the value of the tree? This is the vital question to the man who invests money, time, or labor in the enterprise, and the question I have aimed to answer.

In treating of forest-planting I have, to some extent, done nothing more than give the opinions of great writers on the subject, and in their own language.

The sources of original ideas in any subject are few. I have, therefore, thought it wiser to copy than give anything of my own, less impressive.

In a short essay the subject could not be handled with anything like completeness, and in gathering together fragments from the writings of Franklin B. Hough, the Hon. Geo. P. Marsh, Prof. Lovoe, and others, I have selected that which I thought most valuable, having in view but the one purpose — to present something to the public that would impress them with the importance of this industry.

In the investigation I learned, through my correspondence with the Hon. Thos. Adamson, Jr., United States Consul-general at Melbourne, that Baron Ferd. von Mueller, of Australia, had published several pamphlets on the "*Eucalyptus-trees, and the Importance of Forest Culture*," but that a copy could not be obtained. Mr. Adamson, however, wrote that the Baron would send the copies in his possession provided I would have them published at my own risk, in a connected form. I have deemed the subject of so great and vital importance that I present to the public, in this book, a part of the writings of this valuable author:

First.—"Descriptions of Thirty-two Varieties of the *Eucalypti* Family."

Second.—"Forest Culture in its Relations to Industrial Pursuits."

Third.—"Application of Phytology to the Industrial Purposes of Life."

Fourth.—"Australian Vegetation."

I have in addition to the above the following, which will soon appear in a separate volume :

First.—"The Trees of Australia, Phytologically Named and Arranged, with Indications of their Territorial Distribution."

Second.—"The Principal Timber-trees Readily Eligible for Victorian Industrial Culture, with Indications of their Native Countries, and some of their Technologic Uses."

Third.—"Select Plants (exclusive of timber-trees) Readily Eligible for Victorian Industrial Culture, with Indications of their Native Countries and Some of their Uses."

Fourth.—"Additions to 'Select Plants.'"

Fifth.—"Second Supplement to the 'Select Plants.'"

Sixth.—"The objects of a Botanic Garden in Relation to Industries."

ELLWOOD COOPER.

FOREST CULTURE

AND

Australian Gum Trees:

A LECTURE

(Third of a Series)

Delivered by ELLWOOD COOPER,

NOVEMBER 26TH, 1875, BEFORE THE SANTA BARBARA COLLEGE ASSOCIATION.

"The presence of stately ruins in solitary deserts is conclusive proof that great climatic changes have taken place within the period of human history, in many eastern countries, once highly cultivated and densely peopled, but now arid wastes.

"Although the records of geology teach that great vicissitudes of climate, from the torrid and humid conditions of the coal period to those of extreme cold which produced the glaciers of the drift, may have in turn occurred in the same region, we have no reason to believe that any material changes have been brought about, by astronomical or other natural causes, within the historic period. We cannot account for the changes that have occurred since these sunburnt and sterile plains, where these traces of man's first civilization are found, were clothed with a luxuriant vegetation, except by ascribing them to the improvident acts of man in destroying the trees and plants which once clothed the surface and sheltered it from the sun and the winds. As this shelter was removed the desert approached, gaining new power as its area increased, until it crept over vast regions once populous and fertile, and left only the ruins of former magnificence."

"There are parts of Asia Minor, of Northern Africa, of Greece, and even of Alpine Europe, where the operation of causes set in action by man has brought the face of the earth to a desolation almost as complete as that of the moon. And though, within the brief space of time men call the '*historical period*,' they are known to have been covered with luxuriant woods, verdant pastures, and fertile meadows, they are now too far deteriorated to be reclaimable by man. Nor can they become again fitted for human use except through great geological changes, or other mysterious influences or agencies of which we have no present knowledge, and over which we have no prospective control. The earth is fast becoming an unfit home for its noblest inhabitants, and another era of equal human crime and human improvidence, and of like duration with that through which traces of that crime and improvidence extend, would reduce it to such a condition of impoverished productiveness, of shattered surface, of climatic excess, as to threaten the depravation, barbarism, and perhaps even extinction of the species."

"In European countries, especially in Italy, Germany, Austria, and France, where the injuries resulting from the cutting off of timber have long since been realized, the attention of governments has been turned to this subject by the necessities of the case, and conservative measures have, in many instances, been successfully applied, so that a supply of timber has been obtained, by cultivation, and other benefits resulting from this measure have been realized."

In these countries there are over two dozen schools of forestry, where special instruction is imparted to the youth who are to take the future care of the public forests and private plantations.

The attention of our Government was called to the importance of reserving timber for our navy, and an Act was passed March 1, 1817, making reservations of public lands for this purpose. This Act, however, proved ineffectual, and has a long time since been disregarded, and there is nothing at the present time to prevent the complete destruction of every wooded spot in the country.

"The preservation of forests is one of the first interests of society, and consequently one of the first duties of government. All the wants of life are closely related to their preservation; agriculture, architecture, and almost all the industries seek therein their aliment and resources, which nothing could replace.

"Necessary as are the forests to the individual, they are not less so to the state. It is from thence that commerce finds the means of transportation and exchange, and that governments claim the elements of their protection, their safety, and even their glory.

"It is not alone from the wealth which they offer by their working, under wise regulation, that we may judge of their utility. Their existence is of itself of incalculable benefit to the countries that possess them, as well in the protection and feeding of the springs and rivers as in their prevention against the washing away of the soil upon mountains, and in the beneficial and healthful influence which they exert upon the atmosphere.

"Large forests deaden and break the force of heavy winds that beat out the seeds and injure the growth of plants; they form reservoirs of moisture; they shelter the soil of the fields, and upon hill-sides, where the rain-waters, checked in their descent by the thousand obstacles they present by their roots and the trunks of trees, have time to filter into the soil and only find their way by slow degrees to the rivers. They regulate, in a certain degree, the flow of the waters and the hygrometrical condition of the atmosphere, and their destruction accordingly increases the duration of droughts and gives rise to the injuries of inundations, which denude the face of the mountains.

"The destruction of forests has often become to the country where this has happened a real calamity and a speedy cause of approaching decline and ruin. Their injury and reduction below the degree of present or future wants is among the misfortunes which we should provide against, and one of those errors which nothing can excuse, and which nothing but centuries of perseverance and privation can repair.

"But there is another and more cheering era in this history. This is when civilization has advanced, and man, under the safeguard of laws, sets about restoring the desolated forest. The cultivation of wood then becomes an art founded upon principles, and pursued for the gratification of taste, or for purposes of utility. Like every one who labors from choice, the planter experiences gratification in his pursuit. The little tree which he places in the ground quickly becomes a part of the landscape around; and thus the taste is gratified almost as soon as the work is done. In a few years more his woods yield shelter from the winds, and thus increase the value of the lands around, while it is rarely beyond the expectations of human life to look for a direct profit from the wood as it advances to maturity. To expend capital on planting, indeed, is merely to lay out a fund to increase at interest. Planting, then, may be readily rendered the means, on the part of a landed proprietor, of setting aside a fund for any specific purpose—as for a provision for a family; and no man is deemed peculiarly disinterested who merely obeys a dictate of reason and humanity and provides for his descendants. The planter, then, has his motives of rational interest to justify him in the opinion of those who look only to gain. He lays out his capital with a view to a profitable return. He improves the value of his estate, while, in the practice of his art, he finds the materials of an innocent recreation. It may be questioned whether, in the whole range of rural occupations, one more interesting pursuit presents itself than the superintendence of a growing wood, presenting to the eye at every season new objects of interest and solicitude. Where is the planter who would wish the workmanship of his hands undone, and who does not look with an honest pride on the beautiful creation which, with a generous spirit, he has raised up around him?"

These considerations present a problem not difficult of solution—possibly difficult to educate land-owners of their truthfulness.

We must make the people familiar with the facts and the necessities of the case. It must come to be understood that a tree or a forest planted is an investment of capital, increasing annually in value as it grows, like money at interest, and worth at any time what it has cost, including the expense of planting and the interest which this money would have earned at the given date. The great masses of our rural population and land-owners should be inspired with correct ideas as to the importance of planting and preserving trees, and taught the profits that may be derived from planting waste spots with timber, where nothing else would grow to advantage. They should learn the increased value of farms which have the roadsides lined with avenues of trees, and should understand the worth of the shelter which belts of timber afford to fields, and the general increase of wealth and beauty which the country would realize from the united and well-directed efforts of the owners of land in thus enriching and beautifying their estates.

The demand for lumber increases in the United States at the rate of twenty-five per cent. per annum. The decrease of forests is at the rate of 7,000,000 acres annually. Few people have any idea of the immense value of the wood which is used for purposes generally considered unimportant. The fences of the United States are now valued at $1,800,000,000, and it costs, annually, $98,000,000 to keep them in repair. By far the greatest proportion of these are wood. The railroads of the United States use 150,000,000 of ties annually.

There are establishments manufacturing articles of wood alone, numbering 118,684, employing 7,440,000 persons, and using wood valued at $554,000,000 annually.

A seventy-four gun ship swallows up no less than 150,000 cubic feet, requiring 2,000 large, well-grown timber trees. Supposing these trees should stand thirty-three feet apart, it would require the timber of fifty acres to build one such ship.

According to a statistical table published by our Government in 1874, there was in the New England, Middle, and Western States an average of thirty-three per cent. of wooded land. "In France and Germany it has been estimated that at least one fifth of the land should be planted with forest trees in order to maintain the proper hygrometric and electric equilibrium for successful farming." "Mirabeau estimated that there should be retained in France thirty-two per cent. of land in wood." In the State of Texas, it is represented that there is an area four times that of the State of Pennsylvania, without a tree or a shrub. In California there is only $4\frac{1}{10}$ per cent. It is to *this* State I call your attention, and to *this* people my lecture is directed. We have, perhaps, the most healthful, most equable, the best climate on this globe, and the only objections that can be urged are the prevailing high wind, and an uncertain, as well as an insufficient, quantity of rain-fall. Moderate the winds, increase the rain, and we have perfection. This result is so easily and so quickly to be obtained that it ought to have the attention and serious consideration of every land-owner in the State. How is this to be done? How are we to obtain this result? By planting forest trees. I would recommend belts from 100 to 150 feet in width, each quarter of a mile, planted at right angles with the prevailing direction of the winds, and to line all the highways, parallel with or to the general currents, with belts of two or three rows, closely planted. This planting would occupy about one eighth of the land. Then again, it would be particularly desirable to plant all the banks of gulches, four or five rows on either side, in order to prevent further washing; also, all steep side-hills inconvenient to cultivate, or any waste lands that are non-producing. Trees will grow in places where nothing else can be cultivated. A soil too coarse and meager for the cereals may be marvelously productive in forest growth. Ravines and slopes too steep for any other useful product are the favorite seats of timber. Taking belts of land situated similarly to that part of Santa Barbara county lying between Point Conception, Rincon Point, the Santa Inez Mountains, and the ocean, if planted as above, fully one fourth would be occupied by trees. It is known and proved that the three fourths of the surface will produce more, if protected by trees planted on the other fourth, than the whole would without the trees, and without the protection. Consequently the possessor loses nothing in the productiveness of his farm, but, on the contrary, he increases the certainty of his crops, decreases one fourth his labor, beautifies his home, improves the climate, doubles the value of his land, receives inspiration from this work of his own hands, elevates his own condition, and adds to the refinement of himself, his family, and all his surroundings.

By reason of the mildness of the climate and the discovery of the *Eucalyptus*, or what is known as Australian Gum-tree, we can, in our generation, create forests of these trees, and bring about all these conditions to be enjoyed by ourselves. No other country is so susceptible ; to no other country can we look for equal results.

* The *Eucalyptus globulus* (known as the Blue Gum, and so generally admired in California) is a native of Tasmania. It has received the name *Eucalyptus* on account of the formation of the seed-pods. The name is from two Greek words, signifying "I conceal well," the cup for a long time concealing the stamens. The name *globulus* was taken from the resemblance to a button. The discovery was made by a French botanist by the name of Labillardiere. This gentleman was a member of a French expedition, fitted out in 1791, and, quoting from his journal: "12th May, 1792. [The expedition was then in the port of Entrecasteaux, in the Bay of Tempests, Van Dieman's Land.] I have not yet been able to procure the flowers of a new species of *Eucalyptus*, remarkable for its fruit, which resembles a coat-button. This tree, which is one of the tallest in nature, since it measures upward of one hundred and sixty feet, only blooms toward its upper extremity. The wood is suited to naval construction, and is durable, but neither so light nor so elastic as pine. This beautiful tree, of the myrtle family, is covered with a smooth bark ; the branches bend a little as they rise, and are garnished at the extremities with alternate leaves, slightly curved, and about seven inches in length and nearly two in width. The flowers are solitary, and grow out of the axils of the leaves. The bark, leaves, and fruit are aromatic, and might be employed for economical uses, in place of those which the Moluccas have hitherto exclusively furnished us." "In the history of the

* Copied from the translation from the French of Prof. J. E. Planchon.

future naturalization of the *Eucalyptus* Mueller is the *savant* who justly calculated the future of the tree, traced it in its itineracy, and predicted its destiny. Ramel is the enthusiastic amateur who has thrown body and mind into the mission of propagating it. Both have faith; but one is a prophet, the other an apostle, and, in the noble confraternity of services, public gratitude will not separate the names that are bound together by friendship." "The *Eucalyptus globulus*, known as the Blue Gum, was introduced into Algeria in 1854, while its name and properties were unknown. It is now being planted by hundreds of thousands, in groves, in avenues, in groups, in isolated stalks, in every section of three provinces." A colonist and ardent planter, M. Trottier, regarded this tree as possessing a forest substance capable one day of enriching the colony, and he took for the motto of one of his writings the following: "The wood of the *Eucalyptus* will be the great product of Algeria." Carrying his confidence still further, he saw the desert retreating before this colonized tree, and, speculating upon the incontestible fact that the forest created humidity and changed the hygrometrical *régime* of a country, and remembering, besides, the subterraneous sheets of water beneath the arid surface of this region, he boldly named another pamphlet "*The Wooded Desert and Colonies*," thus conceiving the idea that the great SAHARA DESERT could be reclaimed by planting this tree. He estimated the profits from planting the *Eucalyptus* in the colonies of Algeria to be from one thousand stalks, in five years, to yield a gross revenue of $240, and $10,650 in twenty-six years. He based the estimate on the annual growth, from actual measurement, of four and one half inches in circumference yearly. At Hamma and at Cannes, near Algiers, the growth in height of young trees averages nineteen inches per month. A stalk one year old, planted in May, attained the height of nineteen feet the following December; the year after it grew nineteen feet; the year after it grew nineteen feet; the latter part of the third year this impulse diminished, but, at the end of fifteen years, the tree was over seventy feet in height.

At "Ellwood," my home, twelve miles west of Santa Barbara, I have growing about fifty thousand trees. The oldest were transplanted in February, three years ago. These trees, however, have not done so well as those planted one year later, for the reason that the roots were too much confined — the transplanting delayed too long. The best growth obtained, under the most favorable circumstances, is a tree growing near my house, three years and one or two months from the seed. Transplanted two years and ten months, is nine and one half inches in diameter and forty-two feet six inches high. There is another tree near by, same age, transplanted at the same time, not so large in the trunk, but has attained the height of forty-five feet six inches, equal to forty-seven hundredths of an inch per day, fourteen and seven nineteenths inches per month, and, in order to attain a height of four hundred feet, would have to continue on growing at this rate for twenty-eight years. Nine and one half inches in diameter for three years and two months is equal to three inches yearly, or nine and forty-three hundredths in circumference yearly. To make a tree sixteen feet in diameter would have to continue on growing in the same ratio for sixty-four years. My last planting was June 25th. The seeds were sown six months before. These trees were purposely kept back — stunted, I may say — as I desired to transplant them only after the disappearance of grasshoppers. From the 25th of June these trees, averaging six to eight inches in height, have now reached six feet (or a great many of them) in the short space of five months. The greatest possible results have been obtained on every part of my place. I have experimented on two steep hill-sides, so stony and rocky that plowing or preparing the ground was impossible; putting them in with a pick, without water, and after the rains were over. On one hill-side I cultivated with the hoe as best I could; on the other did nothing—the mustard, in some places, growing up around the trees seven to eight feet high. The trees cultivated have done very much better than the others. Whether this kind of planting is practicable can only be determined at the end of the next year.

It is claimed for the *Eucalyptus* that it resists Summer dryness, and profits by the rains of the Autumn, Winter, and Spring, wherever the mildness of the climate permits it to vegetate without interruption. I have made no other special observations with regard to the growth of this tree, excepting on Gen. Naglee's place, in San Jose, where I found trees, ten years old, eighteen inches in diameter, and, I should think, eighty to ninety feet high. "Many species of the *Eucalyptus* are, in their native country, truly gigantic trees. A *Eucalyptus colossea* has measured nearly four hundred feet in height, and a *Eucalyptus amygdalina* from four hundred and sixteen to four hundred and seventy-one feet. One of the latter species has reached the height of five hundred feet, which is twenty feet higher than the Pyramid of Cheops, the tallest structure in the world. This tree would cast a shadow upon the summit of the great Pyramid. A giant *Eucalyptus* of Tasmania was not less than thirty feet in diameter near the soil, the height being about three hundred feet.

Without expecting such vast proportions in general, the *Eucalyptus globulus* is not the less the largest forest-tree in the world — excepting only the "*Sequoia Gigantea*," or Big Tree of California. "In its juvenile state it is a finished type of elegance. In its adult period, it is a magnificent representation of strength." The trunk can supply immense planks. One was sent to the London Exhibition, in 1862, measuring seventy-five feet in length, and about ten feet in width. Australia desired to send a plank one hundred and sixty-five feet long, but no ship could be found to transport it. The English Navy begins to appreciate the wood for its solidity, durability, and tenacity. The best whale-ships that furrow the South American Seas are those of Hobart Town; the keels of which are made of the *Eucalyptus globulus*. The wood of the *Eucalyptus* combines density of texture with rapidity of growth. This growth is particularly rapid during its juvenile period, but it does not cease to grow in height until it is twenty-four years old. After this age, the trunks, which are generally very straight, only increase in diameter. Compact and tenacious, the wood, owing to the presence of resinous materials, possesses a sort of incorruptibility, which allows it to remain a long time in contact with salt water. It is equally durable in the ground as is the Oak, and can be employed with advantage for sleepers for railroads. The durability of the wood makes it valuable for the keels of vessels, for the construction of bridges, piers, and viaducts.

"The *Eucalyptus* is not only valuable as a wood, but has medicinal properties. In Valencia, Spain, it is vulgarly called the fever-tree, on account of its properties for preventing malarial fevers. There, its properties are so well known as a cure for fevers that its leaves are often plundered, and in a public garden of a great city, it is necessary to surround the fever-tree with a guard, in order to preserve it from being stripped. It has, also, disinfectant virtues, and is antiseptic for wounds—its essential oil being a stimulant, and the tannin in the leaves, acting as a tonic astringent applied exteriorly, hastens the healing of a wound. Various chemists have enumerated its uses as an infusion, decoction, powder, distilled water, tincture, extract and essence. From the most authentic testimony, the *Eucalyptus* appears or seems to be a very efficacious remedy against a great number of intermittent fevers.

"**Eucalyptus globulus*, Blue Gum-tree of Victoria and Tasmania. This tree is of extremely rapid growth, and attains a height of four hundred feet, furnishing a first-class wood. Ship-builders get keels of this timber one hundred and twenty feet long; besides this, they use it extensively for planking and many other parts of the ship, and it is considered to be generally superior

* Thos. Adamson, Jr., U. S. Consul-General at Melbourne, copied at my request from the pamphlets of Baron Ferd. von Mueller, the description here given to the *E. globulus*, and *E. rostrata*.

to American Rock Elm. A test of strength has been made between some Blue Gum, English Oak, and Indian Teak. The Blue Gum carried fourteen pounds weight more than the Oak, and seventeen and one fourth pounds more than Teak upon the square inch. Blue Gum wood, besides being used for ship-building, is very extensively used by carpenters for all kinds of out-door work; also, for fence-rails, railway sleepers—lasting about nine years—for shafts and spokes of drays, and a variety of other purposes."

Eucalyptus rostrata, the Red Gum of Victoria, South Australia, and many river-flats in the interior of the Australian Continent. Although a native tree of this colony, it has been introduced into this list on account of its wood being of extraordinary endurance under ground, and, for this reason, so highly valued for fence-posts, piles, and railway sleepers; for the latter purpose it will last at least a dozen years, and, if well-selected, much longer.

It is also extensively used by ship-builders * * *. It should be steamed before it is worked for planking. Next to the *Jarrah*, from West Australia, this is the best wood for resisting the attacks of sea-worms and white ants. For other details of this and other native trees I refer to the report of the Victorian Exhibition of 1862 and 1867.

The tree attains a height of fully one hundred feet. The supply for our local wants already falls short, and it cannot be obtained from Tasmania, where the tree does not naturally exist."

In my correspondance with Mr. T. W. Herkimer, who lived ten years in Australia and Tasmania, spending about half the time in each place, and variously engaged in mining, wood-cutting lumbering, constructing telegraph lines, etc., etc., I have learned the following: That the general character of the country, the climate, the quantity of rain-fall—except that they may have a little more rain in Summer in Australia and Tasmania, where the Gum Trees grow—is very similar to the Redwood districts of California; the growth being more rapid and the trees larger in the coast ranges, ravines, and valleys than in any other localities—the nearer the foot of the ranges the better. The thicker they are planted, and the thick- they grow, the better, as they will shade each other. I have always noticed that all trees grow taller and straighter where they grow close together. "All trees grown on an open plain, exposed to the sun and wind, will not grow tall, like they do in the forest, where they are protected and shaded. I have seen, in Australia and Tasmania, Blue Gums larger and taller than I have seen Redwood; many of the Gum Trees from fourteen to sixteen feet in diamater, perfectly sound, and, I think, three hundred feet high. The Blue Gum, if it could be grown so as to make large trees, I think, is the most useful, for it is not only good for posts and rails, but ties and piles. While I was in Tasmania there was a test made as to the value for war purposes. It was found that a cannon-ball would pierce the planks, cutting a round hole, and passing through, without splitting the planks. The experiments were so satisfactory that the wood was pronounced as good as English Oak.

"I was appointed to superintend the construction of a telegraph line from the river Lamar, on the north coast of Tasmania, to Hobart Town, on the south coast. We used for poles the young trees of the Blue Gum, White Gum, Red Gum, and Stringy-bark, taking only the bark off. We charred the butts as far as they went into the ground, and dipped in coal-tar. They were expected to last ten or twelve years. When I finished the construction of the telegraph line I was engaged in a saw-mill on the river Mersey. The timber that we sawed was, as above mentioned, Blue, White, and Red Gum and Stringy-bark; we sawed it for all purposes used in house-building, except rustic and siding. It is used in large quantities for piles, wharf, and bridge building. The timber-dealers in Melbourne, and all other ports, do not make a difference in contracting for a cargo of lumber of colonial woods. It is generally expected that it will be mixed. Wheelrights always select the Blue Gum, it being considered much better for wagon-making than most other varieties; it is stronger and more durable, and quite equal to the Hickory of this country. It is used for axletrees, hubs, spokes, and all parts of the running-gear. The Blue Gum is much tougher and heavier, and will last longer than any of the others; in fact, it will last a life-time if taken from large trees. The wood resembles the Rock Elm of the Eastern States. I have rafted a great deal of it; when thrown into the water green will nearly always sink to the bottom, so that it is necessary to lash the rafts alongside of boats to keep them on the surface. A pile sixty feet long, fifteen inches in diameter, will require the strength of two men to raise to the surface. It weighs sixty-seven pounds to the cubic foot.

"The Stringy-bark tree has a leaf the same as the Blue Gum, and is known in the Australian Colonies as the Gum Top Stringy-bark.

"The Stringy-bark tree has a very thick bark on the trunk, and of the same color as the bark of the Redwood. The Blue, White, and Red Gums, after they become large trees, shed their bark, which grows in growths, the outside layers, too small for the inner, crack open, the wind gets between the growths, tears it off in strips three or four inches wide, and sometimes one hundred feet long; the debris covering the ground at the trunk five or six feet in depth.

"The Iron-bark tree does not grow in Tasmania; it is an Australian tree; has a rough bark, something like the bark of the Black Oak of Canada. The bark and the wood are very hard and heavy; will sink in water, like a stone; will last for years; in fact, I do not believe it will ever rot. The largest trees of this variety I have seen were not over four feet in diameter."

Mr. Casey of Melbourne recommends the *Eucalyptus rostrata* as being of great value, more hardy than the Blue Gum, and possessing all the sanitary properties, capable of a high polish, and specially adapted for piles and for ship-timber.

The *Eucalyptus globulus*, or Blue Gum, is a very tender plant when young. It is an evergreen of rapid growth, and the young shoots are injured by a few degrees of frost. It is reported that trees have been destroyed by cold at New Orleans after reaching a height of fifteen feet.

I have selected from the one hundred to one hundred and fifty species of the Eucalypti family the following varieties: *Eucalyptus globulus*, *E. rostrata*, *E. marginata*, *E. syderoxylon*, *E. brachypoda*, *E. obliqua*, *E. platyphilla*, *E. phonicea*, and *E. amygdalina*.*

* The description as given in the lecture is omitted in this place, as it appears more fully on pages 32 to 39.

Propagation.—My plan of germinating the seeds and transplanting to permanent sites is as follows: I have found, from repeated experiments, that it is better to germinate the seeds in boxes, a convenient size for handling, say two and one half to three feet square and six inches deep, placing first about four inches of good sandy soil or loam; then about one inch of pure sand (I use sea sand), and cover the sand with sawdust made from dry or well-seasoned wood, about one inch deep. Plant the seeds in the sawdust half an inch deep or more; thoroughly wet the whole, and keep the top moist. If the seeds are fresh and good they will sprout and come through on the eighth day. I have found no difficulty in sprouting them in the open air during the months of August, September, and October. It is, however, better to raise them under glass—the greater the heat the better success; but as soon as fairly up, put out in the air and sunlight. In six to eight weeks after the seeds are planted the trees will be large enough for transplanting to permanent sites. There is no time that they can be handled with equal success as when about six weeks old, or four to six inches high. The earth or place in which to be planted should be well cultivated, the soil smooth and free from clods, the trees set out just before rain, or in the evenings with a little water, the ordinary care required for setting out cabbage-plants will prove successful with the little Blue Gum plants. It is, however, better to take advantage of approaching rains. I have, with ten men, transplanted as many as seven thousand in an afternoon, and have ninety-five per cent. live. The above plan of transplanting is only practicable during the rainy season. If the ground is well cultivated during the Winter and kept entirely clean the trees can be transplanted at any time during the Summer or dry season. To do this, however, it will be necessary to transplant from boxes where germinated into other boxes, allowing about three inches square of soil and six inches deep, for each little tree, so that the soil with tree can be placed in the ground where they are permanently to grow, without disturbing or exposing the roots. There should be about half a bucket of water to each tree—the water put into the hole, and immediately after it disappears the tree set in.

It is estimated of the Blue Gum that there are fifty thousand seeds in one pound, and that forty thousand will grow, being equal to two thousand five hundred to the ounce.

Eucalyptus rostrata, or Red Gum.—There are, of this variety, at least double the number, and equal to five thousand trees to the ounce. The plan of germinating the seeds of this tree is very similar to that of the Blue Gum, excepting that there must be not over half the quantity of sawdust, and no sand required ; the seeds planted nearer the surface, and more heat necessary. The manner of transplanting the same as the Blue Gum.

I recommend in forest-planting that the trees be set six to seven feet apart, and in rows, where it is possible, so as to cultivate with a horse, while the trees are small. Six by seven will give one thousand trees to the acre. After five years' growth remove three fourths of them, leaving about two hundred and fifty of the straightest and best trees. My estimate of income from the three fourths to be thinned out is as follows:

Seven hundred fence-posts, worth	$100
Cord wood, worth	100
	$200
Expense preparing and marketing	100

Profits $100, equal to $20 each year, and better than barley crops, with all the value left on the ground. At the end of fifty years the two hundred and fifty trees left standing would be worth $10,000, and equivalent to one hundred per cent. profit on the investment, allowing the land to be worth $100 per acre, and interest compounded at ten per cent. per year. M. Trottier's estimate gives as much in half the number of years.

The estimate of profit on one acre of White Ash, in the Western States, at the end of twelve years, is $600.

The measurement of trees in Springfield, Ohio, twenty years' growth, one foot above the ground: Larch, 10½ inches; Birch, 10⅓; Elm, 14⅓; Spruce, 14; Burr Oak, 15. They are planting in the Prairie States one hundred and fifty million trees annually, occupying about two hundred thousand acres, and equal to about *one thirty-fifth* of the destruction throughout the entire country.

Humboldt, the great philosopher, said: "Men, in all climates, seem to bring upon future generations two calamities at once—a want of fuel and a scarcity of water."

A blessing has been pronounced upon the man who would make two blades of grass grow in place of one. How much more is this due to the man who plants a tree where nothing grew before.

Taking in view the conditions so favorable for tree-planting in California, and the great necessity of forest protection, the only wonder is that something as I have suggested was not commenced several years ago. The reasons are so many and so obvious that there is not a question as to the necessity; and if a necessity, it becomes the duty of every land-owner to begin at once to plant trees. It is also clear that in whatever it is our duty to act it is our duty to study. I have therefore thought it worth while to present to you in this lecture a few sketches, which cannot but prove useful till they give place to something better. If the effort creates in the minds of the people an interest in the subject, all that could be hoped for will be accomplished. No one disputes the importance of planting on the plan suggested; neither can the feasibility be questioned. Contemplate the beauty, the grandeur, the productiveness of the great valleys of the Sacramento, the San Joaquin, the Salinas plain, and of every strip of arable land in the State, with belts of *Eucalyptus*-*trees* planted as I have recommended. With such shelter California would become the paradise of the world.

How is this to be brought about? By convincing owners of land that financially it will be a great success. Individual effort alone must accomplish the work. We cannot look to the State for either aid or protection, as, in this *independent*, *free Republic*, the Government or the State is powerless in the execution of any measure that would compel land-owners to plant trees, no matter how urgent the necessity or how important the duty. What we have therefore to do, as individuals, is to begin at once to plant. It is an obligation we owe to the possessory title to land; and financially we will be amply rewarded for our labors.

The following I have copied from a pamphlet, entitled "The Principal Timber-Trees Readily Eligible for Victorian Industrial Culture," by Baron Ferd. von Mueller. (The same offered to the Victorian Acclimation Society—pages 20, 21, and 22):

EUCALYPTUS AMYGDALINA (Labill.). — In our sheltered, springy forest glens, attaining not rarely a height of over four hundred feet, there forming a smooth stem and broad leaves, producing also seedlings of a foliage different to the ordinary state of *Euc. amygdalina*, as occurs in more open country. This species or variety, which might be called *Eucalyptus regnous*, represents the loftiest tree in British territory, and ranks next to the *Sequoia Wellingtonia* in size anywhere on the globe. The wood is fissile, well adapted for shingles, rails, for house-building, for the keelson and planking of ships, and other purposes. Labillardiere's name applies ill to any of the forms of this species. Seedlings raised on rather barren ground near Melbourne have shown the same amazing rapidity of growth as those of the *Euc. globulus;* yet, like those of *Euc. obliqua*, they are not so easily satisfied with any soil.

EUCALYPTUS CITRIODORA (Hooker).—Queensland. It combines with the ordinary qualities of many Eucalypts the advantage of yielding from its leaves a rather large supply of volatile oil, of excellent lemon-like fragrance.

EUCALYPTUS DIVERSICOLOR (F. v. Mueller).—The Karri of S. W. Australia. A colossal tree, exceptionally reaching to the height of four hundred feet, with a proportionate girth of the stem. The timber is excellent. Fair progress of growth is shown by the young trees, planted even in dry, exposed localities in Melbourne. The shady foliage and dense growth of the tree promise to render it one of our best for avenues. In its native localities it occupies fertile, rather humid valleys.

EUCALYPTUS GLOBULUS (Labill.).—Blue Gum of Victoria and Tasmania. This tree is of extremely rapid growth, and attains a height of four hundred feet, furnishing a first-class wood. Ship-builders get keels of this timber one hundred and twenty feet long; besides this, they use it extensively for planking, and many other parts of the ship, and it is considered to be generally superior to American Rock Elm. A test of strength has been made between some Blue Gum, English Oak, and Indian Teak. The Blue Gum carried fourteen pounds weight more than the Oak, and seventeen pounds four ounces more than Teak, upon the square inch. Blue Gum wood, besides being used for ship-building, is very extensively used by carpenters for all kinds of out-door work; also, for fence-rails, railway-sleepers—lasting about nine years—for shafts and spokes of drays, and a variety of other purposes.

EUCALYPTUS GOMPHOCEPHALA (Candolle).—The Tooart of S. W. Australia. Attains a height of fifty feet. The wood is close-grained, hard, and not rending. It is used for ship-building, wheelwright's work, and other purposes of artisans.

EUCALYPTUS MARGINATA (Smith).—The Jarrah or Mahogany tree of S. W. Australia, famed for its indestructible wood, which is attacked neither by chelura, nor teredo, nor termites, and therefore so much sought for jetties and other structures exposed to sea-water; also for any underground work, and largely exported for railway sleepers. Vessels built of this timber have been enabled to do away with all copper-plating. It is very strong, of a close grain and a slightly oily and resinous nature. It works well, makes a fine finish, and is by ship-builders here considered superior to either Oak, Teak, or, indeed, any any other wood. The tree grows chiefly on iron-stone ranges.

At Melbourne it is not quick of growth, if compared to our Blue Gum (*Euc. globulus,* Lab.), or to our Stringy-bark (*E. obliqua,* 'l Her.), but it is likely to grow with celerity in our ranges.

EUCALYPTUS ROSTRATA (Schlechtendal).*—The Red Gum of Victoria, South Australia, and many river-flats in the interior of the Australian continent. Although a native tree of this colony, it has been introduced into this list on account of its wood being of extraordinary endurance under ground, and for this reason so highly valued for fence-posts, piles, and railway sleepers; for the latter purpose it will last at least a dozen years, and if well-selected, much longer. It is also extensively used by ship-builders, for main stem, stern-post, inner post, deadwood, floor timbers, futtocks, transoms, knight-head, hawse-pieces, cant, stern, quarter and fashion timber, bottom-planks, breast-hooks, and riders, windlass, bow-rails, etc., etc. It should be steamed before it is worked for planking. Next to the Jarrah, from West Australia, this is the

* Second supplement by the same author. It is said of this variety that instances are on record of the stem having attained a girth of sixty feet, at six feet from the ground, through the formation of buttresses.

best wood for resisting the attacks of sea-worms and white ants. For other details of the uses of this and other native trees, refer to the reports of the Victorian Exhibitions of 1862 and 1867. The trees attain a height of fully one hundred feet. The supply for our local wants falls already short, and cannot be obtained from Tasmania, where the tree does not naturally exist.

EUCALYPTUS SIDEROXYLON (Cunn). — Iron - bark tree. It attains a height of one hundred feet, and supplies a valuable timber, possessing great strength and hardness. It is much prized for its durability by carpenters, ship - builders, etc. It is largely employed by wagon - builders, for wheels, poles, etc. ; by ship-builders for top-sides, tree-nails, the rudder (stock), belaying-pins, and other purposes; it is also used by turners, for rough work. This is considered the strongest wood in our colony. It is much recommended for railway-sleepers, and extensively used in underground mining work.

[Copied from an additional list offered to the same society by the same author, and published by said society in 1874—pages 64, 65, 66, 67, and 68] :

EUCALYPTUS ACMENOIDES (Schauer).—New South Wales and East Queensland. The wood used in the same way as that of *E. obliqua* (the stringy-bark tree), but superior to it. It is heavy, strong, durable, of a light color, and has been found good for palings, flooring-boards, battens, rails, and many other purposes of house carpentry. (Rev. Dr. Woolls.)

EUCALYPTUS BOTRYOIDES (Smith). — From East Gipps Land to South Queensland. One of the most stately among an extensive number of species, remarkable for its dark green shady foliage. It delights on river banks. Stems attain a length of eighty feet without a branch, and a diameter of eight feet. The timber usually sound to the centre, adapted for water work, wagons, knees of boats, etc. Posts of it very lasting, as no decay was observed in fourteen years.

EUCALYPTUS BRACHYPODA (Turczaninow).—Widely dispersed over the most arid extra-tropical as well as tropical inland regions of Australia. One of the best trees for desert tracts; in favorable places one hundred and fifty feet high. Wood brown, sometimes very dark, hard, heavy, and elastic, prettily marked; thus used for cabinet work, but more particularly for piles, bridges, and railway-sleepers. (Rev. Dr. Woolls.)

EUCALYPTUS CALOPHYLLA (R. Brown). — Southwest Australia. More umbrageous than most Eucalypts, and of comparatively rapid growth. The wood is free of resin when grown on alluvial land- but not so when produced on stony ranges. It is preferred to that of *E. marginata* and *E. cornuta* for rafters, spokes, and fence-rails; it is strong and light but not long lasting underground. The bark is valuable for tanning, as an admixture to *Acacia* bark.

EUCALYPTUS CORNUTA (Labillardiere). — Southwest Australia. A large tree, of rapid growth, preferring a somewhat humid soil. The wood is used for various artisans' work, and there preferred for the strongest shafts and frames of carts, and other work requiring hardness, toughness, and elasticity.

EUCALYPTUS CREBRA (F. v. Mueller).—The narrow-leaved iron-bark tree of New South Wales and Queensland. Wood reddish, hard, heavy, elastic, and durable; much used in the construction of bridges; also, of wagons, piles, fencing, etc. *E. melanophloia* (F. v. M.), the silver-leaved iron-bark tree, and *E. leptophleba*, *E. trachyphloia* and *E. drepanphylla* are closely allied species of similar value. They all exude astringent gum-resin in considerable quantity, resembling kino in appearance and property.

EUCALYPTUS DORATOXYLON (F. v. Mueller).—The spear-wood of South-west Australia, where it occurs in sterile districts. The stem is slender and remarkably straight, and the wood of such firmness and elasticity that the nomadic natives wander long distances to obtain it as material for their spears.

EUCALYPTUS EUGENIOIDES (Sieber).—New South Wales. Regarded by the Rev. Dr. Woolls as a fully distinct species. Its splendid wood, there, often called Blue Gum-tree wood, available for many purposes, and largely utilized for ship-building.

EUCALYPTUS GUNNII (J. Hooker).—Victoria, Tasmania and New South Wales, at alpine and subalpine elevations. The other more hardy Eucalyptis comprise *E. coriacea*, *E. alpina*, *E. urnigera*, *E. coccifera*, and *E. vernicosa*, which all reach heights covered with snow for several months in the year.

EUCALYPTUS PANICULATA (Smith). —The White Iron-bark tree of New South Wales. All the trees of this series are deserving of cultivation, as their wood, though always excellent, is far from alike, and that of each species preferred for special purposes of the artisans.

EUCALYPTUS PHŒNICEA, (F. v. Muller).—Carpentaria and Arnheim's Land. Of the quality of the timber hardly anything is known, but the brilliancy of its scarlet flowers recommends this species to a place in any forest or garden plantation. For the same reason, also, *E. miniata*, from North Australia, and *E. ficifolia*, from South-west Australia, should be brought extensively under cultivation.

EUCALYPTUS PILULARIS (Smith).—The Black-butt tree of South Queensland, New South Wales, and Gipps Land. One of the best timber-yielding trees about Sydney; of rather rapid growth (Rev. Dr. Woolls). It is much used for flooring-boards.

EUCALYPTUS PLATYPHYLLA (F. v. Mueller.)—Queensland. Regarded by the Rev. Julian Tenison Woods as one of the best of shade-trees, and seen to produce leaves sometimes one and one half feet long, and one foot wide. This tree is available for open, exposed localities, where trees from deep forest valleys would not thrive.

EUCALYPTUS ROBUSTA (Smith).—New South Wales. The timber in use for ship-building, wheelwright's work, and many implements, such as mallets, etc.

EUCALYPTUS RESINIFERA (Smith).—The Red Mahogany Eucalypt of South Queensland and New South Wales. A superior timber-tree, according to the Rev. Dr. Woolls, the wood being much prized for its strength and durability.

EUCALYPTUS SIDEROPHLOIA (Bentham).—The large-leaved or red Iron-bark tree of New South Wales and South Queensland. According to the Rev. Dr. Woolls, this furnishes one of the strongest and most durable timbers of New South Wales; with great advantage used for railway sleepers, and for many building purposes. It is harder even than the wood of *E. sideroxylon*, but thus also worked with more difficulty.

EUCALYPTUS TERETICORNS (Smith).—From East Queensland to Gipps Land. Closely allied to *E. rostrata* and seemingly not inferior to it in value.

EUCALYPTUS TESSELARIS (F. v. Mueller).—N. Australia and Queensland. Furnishes a brown, rather elastic wood, not very hard, available for many kinds of artisan's work, and particularly sought for staves and flooring. The tree exudes much astringent gum resin (P. O'Shanesy). Many other Eucalypts could have been mentioned as desirable for wood culture, but it would have extended this enumeration beyond the limits assigned to it. Moreover, the quality of many kinds is not yet sufficiently ascertained, or not yet fully appreciated even by the artisans and woodmen.

PLANT CATALOGUE,

ANDERSON, HALL & CO., SYDNEY.

N. S. WALES HARDWOOD TIMBER-TREES.

In many respects, no timbers in the world can compare with those of Australia. For all purposes requiring great strength, combined with great durability, they are unapproached. Those of New South Wales have, as a rule, a reputation in those respects superior to those of similar species in the other Australian colonies. This superiority has been noticed more particularly in tougher and closer-packed tissues. So much is this the case that, for some particular purposes, such timber as Iron-bark and Blue Gum have to be obtained from New South Wales for use in Victoria, although both species are common there. Among other peculiarly valuable properties possessed by our timbers, for such purposes as bridges, jetties, or any other buildings where strong timber may be used, not the least is the valuable quality of difficult ignition and lack of inflammability.

Of late years these woods, and the forests which produce them, have attracted a great deal of attention in Europe, not only for the qualities of the timber, but for other properties, which are being from time to time discovered by science, and promising extraordinary riches in both medicine and the arts.

As a fuel, both for domestic and industrial purposes, the wood, natural and carbonized, of some species, is superior to most others, and, for steam purposes, some, as Iron-bark and Box, are only inferior to coal.

Possessing so many valuable qualities, combined with the fact that these trees are found growing, in New South Wales, in boundless forests, under extremes of climate, both as to heat and cold — ranging from one hundred and thirty to twenty-five degrees Fahrenheit—it may be inferred that forests of them will some day be planted in many other parts of the world.

The following list comprises the principal species:

1. White Gum (*Eucalyptus hæmastoma*).—Yields gum resin largely, is not remarkable for its timber, but is a good domestic fuel. Height, fifty to one hundred feet.

2. River White Gum (*E. radiata*).—A fair-lasting timber for rough fencing; difficult to burn; a bad fuel. One hundred feet.

3. Blue Gum, Common Parramatta (*E. rostrata, B.*)—Used in ship-building for knees, beams, and some kinds of planking. A very durable wood; will last well as posts in the ground; inferior fuel. One hundred and twenty feet.

4. Flooded Blue Gum (*E. eugenoides*).—The best timber for ship-building (planking in particular); very durable. One of the best timbers for many purposes; inferior fuel. One hundred and eighty feet.

5. Grey Gum or Red Gum (*E. tereticornis*). — A very strong, durable, hard wood, almost equal to Iron-bark for some purposes; lasts in the ground; inferior fuel. One hundred and fifty feet.

6. Drooping Gum (*E. saligna*). — A medium timber; inferior fuel. One hundred feet.

7. Blue Gum like the Flooded Gum (*E. gonicalyx*). Used in ship-building; is the best wood for felloes in wheels; very durable; inferior fuel. One hundred and fifty feet.

8. Spotted Gum (*E. maculata*). — A very strong, light, and elastic timber, very durable as girders or beams; the best wood for staves, and useful for sawn timber in household carpentry; first-class fuel for domestic use. One hundred and twenty feet.

9. Dark or Broad-leaved Iron-bark (*E. siderophloia*).—The most valuable wood for piles, girders, railway-sleepers, and for every purpose in which strength and durability are required; even shingles of one fourth inch thickness have been known to last sound on roofs for forty years. This species and the two following are the strongest of all Australian timbers, and are used for a greater number of purposes—spokes, shafts, poles, frames, by wheelwrights; the best telegraph-posts, fencing of all kinds, and none are equal to it for cogs in mill-work. It is superior to most as fuel for steam-engines, as it throws off more heat, etc., etc. One hundred and fifty feet.

10. Common Iron-bark (*E. paniculata*).—For most purposes equal to the last species; is less inlocked and is more easily split into shingles or palings; it is as lasting and as good fuel as other Iron-barks; the wood is not so dark in color. One hundred and twenty feet.

11. Small-leaved or She Iron-bark (*E. microphylla*) (?).—The wood of this species is used for fencing and many purposes the same as the other Iron-barks. But the wood being of a nature much more

easy to work, it may be used in carpentry in many ways, to which the hardness of the other sorts offers an obstacle; first-class fuel. One hundred and twenty feet.

12. STRINGY-BARK (*E. obliqua*).—The best wood for flooring-boards, rafters, and sawn stuff generally; it is of very thick growth, inferior fuel, but produces the best charcoal for the forge. One hundred and twenty feet.

13. BLACK-BUTT (*E. pilularis*).—Wood like Stringy-bark, and used for similar purposes. Small spars of this species are used for shipping. It is almost the only Eucalyptus that is used for this purpose; inferior fuel. One hundred and fifty to two hundred feet.

14. YELLOW BLACK-BUTT (*E. obtusiflora*).—Timber like the preceding, but softer and more easily worked, and of a yellow tint. It is a remarkably quick grower. One hundred and fifty feet.

15. COMMON BOX (*E. hemiphloia*).—A hard but useful timber, strong, tough, and durable, but will not last as posts or piles sunk in the ground. It is, also, a first-class fuel both for domestic use and for steam or other industrial purposes. One hundred to one hundred and fifty feet.

16. MESSMATE, OR ALMOND-LEAVED STRINGY-BARK (*E. amygdalina*).—A first-class timber for flooring-boards, joists, and other house-carpentry. It is like Stringy-bark, but the tree is an ace larger, and it is not so generally distributed. It is a bad wood for domestic fuel, but is a first-rate smiths' charcoal. One hundred and fifty to two hundred feet.

17. BLACK BOX (*E. bicolor*).—A highly valued timber-tree; it is equal to the best Iron-bark for all the

purposes for which that wood is used, and is more easily wrought. It is sometimes called "Iron-bark Box." One hundred to one hundred and fifty feet.

18. WOOLLEYBUTT (*E. longifolia*). — An average-sized tree. Fair timber for fencing and building purposes; it is a good fuel for domestic use; very durable, and is said to be less liable to the attack of the white ant than any other of the Eucalypti. One hundred to one hundred and twenty feet.

19. BLOODWOOD (*E. corymbosa*). — A very large tree. Timber first-class for posts, piles, and such like; it is extremely durable in the ground. It is not a favorite as sawn timber, on account of its many gum veins; not a good fuel. One hundred and fifty to two hundred feet.

20. SWAMP MAHOGANY (*E. robusta*).—A good lasting timber for house-carpentry and many kinds of turnery. It is not durable in the ground, but for other purposes it is very durable, and is not a favorite with the white ant. It is not remarkable as a burning wood. Its specific gravity is great. One hundred and fifty feet.

EUCALYPTUS GLOBULUS (*Tasmania Blue Gum*).—In the once despised Gum-tree (*Eucalyptus*) it has been discovered that qualities exist which place it transcendently above any other plants, if not above *all* other plants, in hygienic importance.

By its means large tracts of the very richest land will be made available in many parts of the world. In India, and other parts of Southern Asia, vast areas are left without culture or occupation, overrun with jungle and forest, and totally unfit for man's abode on account of their malaria-producing character. Already has the malaria-destroying exhalations of *Eucalyptus globulus* been practically proved beyond a doubt in Europe, Africa, and America. It is confidently stated that in the fatal Roman Pontine Marshes, and the no less fatal swamps of Lombardy and other parts of Italy, the *Eucalyptus globulus* has rendered healthy, localities in which to sleep a single night was all but certain death.

In America, the Gum-tree is being most extensively planted, with the view of making uninhabitable districts healthy. In fact, so ample are the proofs of its efficacy that millions of malarious acres in all parts of the globe where the climate suits it will, within a very few years, be planted with "Blue Gum."

Eucalyptus globulus has already become noted in all temperate climes as "The Fever-tree," and certain it is that it truly deserves the name. Doubtless other species of *Eucalyptus* possess the same beneficial property, but *globulus* is the only one which has yet been so abundantly tested by practical trial.

It is the easiest of the tribe to rear, and develops from the seedling into the tree with great rapidity. So great has become the demand from Europe and America for seed that the forests of Tasmania are threatened with annihilation. To give our friends some idea of the demand, we sold have nearly half a ton of seed during the past year. One pound weight should produce many thousands of plants; this will give some estimate of the enormous number of trees that must now be planted all over the world.

FOREST CULTURE

IN ITS

RELATIONS TO INDUSTRIAL PURSUITS:

A LECTURE,

DELIVERED BY

Baron Ferd. von Mueller, C.M.G., M.D., Ph.D., F.R.S.

(Government Botanist for Victoria, and Director of the Botanic Gardens of Melbourne),

On the 22d of June, 1871.

" *The toils of science swell the wealth of art.*"
BULWER LYTTON, *from Schiller*.

Strange as it may appear, an impression seems to be prevailing in these communities that our forests have to serve no other purposes but to provide wood for our immediate and present wants, be it fuel or timber. For even after the warning of climatic changes, and after the commencing scarcity of wood, no forest administration, at least none adequate or regularly organized, has been initiated in any portion of Australia; and thus the forests, even in districts already very populous, remain almost unguarded, become extensively reduced, and in some localities are already annihilated; indeed, the requirements of the current time alone are kept in view. Under such circumstances it cannot be surprising that neither an universal forest supervision, nor a judicious restraint of consumption, nor an ample utilization of *all* the various collateral resources of our woodlands, received that serious attention to which such measures became more and more entitled.

During the earlier years of our colonization, while the population was but thinly scattered over the territory, or densely concentrated in a few places only, all demands on the wood resources were comparatively so limited as to cause, perhaps, nowhere vast destruction of the timber vegetation, much less any alarm for meeting the requirements of the future. Then followed the first gold period, with all its bustle, turmoils and agitations, preventing reflection on almost anything except the immediate wants of that stormy time. Subsequently, when the commotion and excitement of the earlier gold era had calmed down, other obstacles arose, which, in their conflicts, brought much sadness on this young country, and retarded for years its full progress. But now, when apparently also these difficulties have been surmounted, it will be all the more incumbent on our statesmen and legislators to exclude no longer from their consideration and watchfulness that remaining portion of a bequest which bountiful Nature, in its rich woods, has intrusted to our care. The maintenance of these forest riches should engage not only the loftiest forethought, but also a well-guided and scrupulous vigilance.

How forests beneficially affect a clime, how they supply equable humidity, how they afford extensive shelter, create springs, and control the flow of rivers—all this the teachings of science, the records of history, and more forcibly still, the sufferings or even ruin of numerous and vast communities, have demonstrated in sad experiences, not only in times long past, but even in very recent periods. In what manner the forests arrest passing miasmata, or set a limit to the spreading of rust-spores from ruined cornfields; in what manner their humid atmosphere and their feathered singers effectually obstruct the march of armies of locusts in the Orient, or hinder the progress of vast masses of acrydia in North America, or oppose the wanderings of other insects elsewhere — all this has been clearly witnessed in our own age. How the forests, as slow conductors of heat, lessen the temperature of warm climes, or banish siroccos; how forests, as ready conductors of electricity, much influence and attract the current of the vapors, or impede the elastic flow of the air, with its storms and its humidity, far above the actual height of the trees, and how they condense the moisture of the clouds by lowering the temperature of the atmosphere, has over and over again been ascertained by many a thoughtful observer. In what mode forests shelter the soil from solar heat, and produce coolness through radiation from the endlessly-multiplied surfaces of their leaves, and through the process of exhalations; how, in the spongy stratum of decaying vegetable remnants, they retain far more humidity than even cultivated soil; how they with avidity re-absorb the surplus of moisture from the air, and refresh by a never-wanting dew all vegetation within them and in their vicinity, has been explained, not only by natural philosophy, but also often by observations of the plainest kind. How forest-trees, by the powerful penetration of their roots, decompose the rocks, and force unceasingly from deep strata the mineral elements of vegetable nutrition to the surface; how they create and maintain the sources for the gentle flow of watercourses for motive power, aqueducts, irrigation, water-traffic and navigation; how they mitigate or prevent malarious influences — of all this we become cognizant by daily experiences almost everywhere around us. We have to look, therefore, far beyond a mere temporary wood supply, when we wish to estimate the blessings of forest vegetation rightly; and our mind has to grasp the complex causes and sequences originating with and depending on the forests, before their value as a total can be understood.

> " Here, in the sultriest season, let us rest:
> Fresh is the green beneath those aged trees;
> Here air of gentlest wing will fan our breast—
> From heaven itself we may inhale the breeze."
>
> BYRON.

Let us then take timely warning; let us remember that denuded earth parts with its warmth by radiation, and is intensely heated by insulation; that thus in woodless countries the extremes of climate are brought about in rendering the Winter-cold far more intense and boisterous, and the Summer-heat far more burning and oppressive. Let us remember why the absence or destruction of forests involves periodic floods and droughts, with all the great disasters inseparable therefrom. Let us bear in mind that even in our praised Australia many a pastoral tenant saw his herds and flocks perish, and even the very kangaroos off his run; how he looked hopefully for months and months at every promising cloud which drew up on the horizon, only to dissolve rainless in the dry desert air; whereas, when the squatter's ruin was completed, the last pasture parched, and the last waterpool dried up, great atmospheric changes would send the rain-clouds over the thirsty land with all the vehemence of precipitation, and would convert dry creeks into foaming torrents, or inundate with furious floods the very pastures over which the carcasses of the famished cattle and sheep were strewn about! Picture to yourselves the ruined occupant of the soil, hardly able to escape with his bare life from the sudden scenes of these tragic disasters! Fortunately, as yet such extreme events may not have happened commonly; yet they did occur, and pronounced their lessons impressively. Let it be well considered that it is not alone the injudicious overstocking of many a pasture, or the want of water-storage, but frequently the very want of rain itself for years in extensive woodless districts, which renders occupation of many of our inland tracts so precarious. Let it also not be forgotten how, without a due proportion of woodland, no country can be great and prosperous! Remember how whole mountain districts of Southern Europe became, with the fall of the forests, utterly depopulated; how the gushes of wide currents washed away all arable soil, while the bordering flat land became buried in debris; how its rivers became filled with sediment, while the population of the lowland were at the same time involved in poverty and ruin! Let us recollect that in many places the remaining alpine inhabitant had to toil with his very fuel for many miles up to the once wooded hills, where barrenness and bleakness would perhaps no longer allow a tree to vegetate! It should be borne in mind that the productiveness of cereal fields is often increased at the rate of fully fifty per cent. merely by establishing plantations of shelter-trees; that the progress of drift-sand is checked by tree-plantations; and that a belt of timber not only affords protection against storms, but also converts sandy wastes finally into arable meadows, thus adding almost unobserved, yet unceasingly, so far to the resources of a country.

Shall we follow, then, the example of those improvident populations who, by clearing of forests, diminished most unduly the annual fall of rain, or prevented its retention; who caused a dearth of timber and fuel, by which not solely the operations of their artisans became already hindered or even paralyzed, but through which even many a flourishing country tract was already converted almost into a desert Should we not rather commence to convert any desert tract into a smiling country, by thinking early and unselfishly of the requirements of those who are to follow us? Why not rather imitate the example set by an Egyptian sovereign, who alone caused, during the earlier part of this century, 20,000,000 of trees to be planted in formerly rainless parts of his dominions.

Dr. H. Rogers, of Mauritius, issued, this year, a report "on the effects of the cutting-down of forests on the climate and health of Mauritius." Still, in 1854, the island was resorted to by invalids from India as the "pearl" of the Indian Ocean, it being then one mass of verdure. When the forests were cleared, to gain space for sugar cultivation, the rainfall diminished even there; the rivers dwindled down to muddy streams; the water became stagnant in cracks, revices, and natural hollows, while the equable temperature of the island entirely changed ; even drought was experienced in the midst of the ocean, and thunder-showers were rarely any longer witnessed. The lagoons, marshes, and swamps along the seaboard were no longer filled with water, but gave off noxious gases ; while the river-waters became impure from various refuse. After a violent inundation, in February, 1865, followed by a period of complete dryness, fever, of a low type, set in, against which the remedies employed in ordinary febrile cases proved utterly valueless. From the waterless sides of the lagoons, pestilential malaria arose, exposed to which the laborers fell on the field, and, in some instances, died within a few hours afterward. But scarcity of good food among the destitute classes, and inadequate sewage arrangement, predisposed also to the dreadful effect of the fever, at the time. As stated by myself, on a former public occasion, marshes should either be fully drained or the means of continuing them submerged should not be withdrawn. Dr. Rogers very properly insists that the plateaux and highlands of Mauritius must be replanted, alone on sanitary reasons. The small island of Malta requires, at this moment, to make strenuous effort for wood culture, to render tillage further possible and the clime more tolerable. The once forest-covered hills, which bordered the rich garden country of Murcia, in Moorish times, are now masses of arid rocks ; while Spain, nowadays, is even helpless to obtain its very fuel, and thus all its technologic industries must languish. No wonder, then, if our here much-disregarded Eucalypts are called there the trees of the future.

But I have, on this occasion, dwelt already long enough on the stern necessity of securing a due relation of forest to territory, of woods to climate, of timber to industries. These great questions have been discussed, by able men, through time long passed, in all countries of civilization. The details, moreover, of such discussions demand a special and fuller teaching, for which, perhaps, opportunities may yet arise in this hall. But to those who wish early to devote fuller attention to vital considerations of this kind, I would recommend the perusal of the admirable work of George P. Marsh (*Man and Nature; or Physical Geography, as modified by Human Action.* London: 1864). That author studied the scattered and largely foreign literature pertaining to this subject with singular care, observed very many original facts, and argued on them with great ability. A smaller, still more recent publication (*Disastrous Effects of the Destruction of Forest Trees in Wisconsin*, by Lapham, Knapp, and Crocker, published in 1867) is also deserving full attention, inasmuch as it brings before us the difficulties and losses which the destruction of the forests has already caused in one of the younger of the American States; while, again, Indian experiences in regard to forests may be traced in the valuable volume issued by Dr. Cleghorn (*Forests of the Punjab and Western Himalaya;* Roor Kee, 1864). Some observations of my own, applying to countries like North Africa, have been recorded two years ago in the *Bulletin de la Societe d' Agriculture d' Alger.*

One of the main objects, however, of my address this evening, is to show in what manner a well-organized and yet inexpensive system of forest administration might check the indiscriminate destruction of the woods, without, perhaps, lessening the rate of the present yield ; in what manner numerous latent industrial resources of our ranges might be speedily and successfully developed, and a higher revenue thus be raised by the state ; in what manner this increased income could be best employed, to maintain or enrich the forests, or to raise woods where naturally none existed ; and by what new means prosperous occupation might be afforded to many a happy family in the still and salubrious sylvan recesses of this country.

And here I would at once remark, that for any administrative organization to watch over our forest interests we must follow an independent path of our own in this young country, because the systems of forest management adopted with so much advantage in Germany, France, and Scandinavia are here applicable only to a very limited extent. This must be at once apparent to any one who will reflect on the disparity which exists between our clime, our native tree vegetation, our present ratio of population and value of labor, as compared with similar conditions of the older and far more densely inhabited countries of middle and northern Europe, not to speak of the very much wider scope which, for the selection of trees for our future use, the isothermal zone of Victoria allows. On the latter subject our Acclimatization Society has recently published the views which I entertain in reference to the many various trees eligible for the geographic latitudes of a colony like ours.* Next I proceed to give, though very briefly, only an outline of the special system of administration, which I would

* Appendix to the Annual Report of the Vict. Acclimat. Soc., 1870-71.

advise to be adopted in the first instance, as well for the supervision, enrichment, and utilization of our native forests as for creating also new ones. On various occasions I have alluded to such a plan of surveillance before. More recently, though only passingly, in a lecture delivered at this hall, I advocated the formation of local Forest Boards in the different districts of our colonial territory. Various considerations led me to recommend this system. The administration, as an honorary one, would involve no direct expenditure to the State. It would bring to bear in each locality special watchfulness and local talent. In each district could readily be found a few inhabitants who not only possess some knowledge of tree-culture in general, but who, also, by their direct interest in the present and future welfare of the locality in which they live, in which they gained experiences, in which they hold property, and in which they reared a family, would be induced, as much for the sake of direct and lasting advantages as from patriotic motives, to devote the needful time for serving on a local Forest Board. But there are still other weighty advantages, which claim support for this proposition. Various tracts of the Victorian territory are—as might be imagined—very unlike in climate and geologic structure. Each locality shows peculiar adaptabilities for special trees to be selected. One district can afford, by the possession of more extensive primeval forests, to be far more heavily taxed in its timber resources than another; one tract of country can produce remuneratively certain trees, which it would be hopeless to attempt raising in another locality. Some extensive areas have no forests at all, and in others they have all but succumbed already. Hence each Forest Board can best frame its own by-laws or local regulations, subject to the approval of ministerial authority; each can best judge of its own particular requirements, not only for the present generation, but also of such as will be urgent at a time when the children and grand-children of the earlier colonists will have to form their judgment on the wisdom or shortcomings of their ancestors here at a time when the want of foresight may fall most crushingly on the vitality or progress of many an industry or even the whole prosperity of the colony, or when, otherwise, the early operations of thoughtful local residents will prove to posterity an incalculable benefit. It will then become apparent whether the present colonists have done their duty to their descendants, and havebeen faithful to the future interests of their adopted country; or whether they sunk all their ideas and efforts in temporary gain, regardless of all consequences. Each forest district, thus guarded by local administrators, will be able to produce a far larger income than now is raised from any of our wood areas; while the removal of timber will be brought within more reasonable bounds, and the wants of the future no longer be disregarded. Means of disposal of the wood, different to the regulations now in force, would be adopted, to save, in places much denuded already of wood, the rest of the timber from complete destruction. Thus, for instance, trees might be sold by numbers at certain sizes, with saving of the youthful trees; or the wood might be removed by the square mile, with a view of replanting. The reckless ringing of trees (merely to obtain a little more grass) and stripping of bark would be brought within stringent laws, and many other losses be obviated.

A gentleman at Hillesley counts, as late as this very month, five splendid trees on an acre, cut down by the splitters, while only about one tenth of the wood is used; nine tenths being left to be swept away, sooner or later, by bush-fires. This improvidence goes on within a few hours' drive from Melbourne. The stately sea-coast Banksias (Banksia integrifolia), so rare near Melbourne, and hardly occurring further westward, have been nearly exterminated within this month, as near to us as Brighton. On all this, local forest surveillance can form far the best opinion. Each Board should have its cultivator, who, simultaneously, could perform the duties of forest-ranger. A few unprovided orphan boys might be occupied in the simple nursery or planting work for the forests. The officer intrusted with forest duties on behalf of the Government might aid, by frequent visits to each forest district, the various Boards with much advice. The expenditure for such an organization in each instance would be most moderate, would be productive already of early remunerative gain, and cause large and immediate savings. No statesman, I feel assured, would wish to impoverish our woods at the expense of the next generation, just as little as any legislator would hesitate to re-vote annually, for each forest administration, at least a portion of the revenue raised from the woods under its control. A sound economy of the State will not expect from a forest in populous localities any more than to devote its means for self-support. One of the first duties devolving on any forest department would undoubtedly be to cause in each district some fertile, sheltered valleys, readily accessible to good lines of traffic, to be selected, where, from springs or rivulets, water could be obtained for inexpensive irrigation, in order to reserve such spots for forest nurseries before they are all alienated from the Crown. The transit of the millions of seedlings needed for forest plantations, from remote spots, would not only be one of enormous and unnecessary expenditure, but, in the many instances of evergreen and even some deciduous trees, it would be next to impossible to convey living plants for long distances. The union of Forest Boards to Road Boards or Shire Councils I regard inadvisable, because their scope of action is so different. The predilections of a member of a municipality will often be in building operations and kindred objects, while for culture processes he may have neither inclination nor experience. It is never wise to burden too heavy responsibilities on a few honorary administrators, whose leisure in this youthful country, where so much work is yet under the first or early process of creating, is almost sure to be but limited.

But there are instances in which—as, indeed, a thoughtful legislator has suggested—the Mining Boards might exercise, in their vicinity, supervision also over the woods. On many professional questions, such as the renovation of forests, the best utilization of their products, the increase of their riches, I would, myself, very gladly afford advice, and thus maintain a consulting position to the Forest Boards; for, need I add, it has ever been my aim to serve, as far as it was within my means, the best interests of my fellow-colonists; and while official responsibility rests on me in this direction, I would wish to meet it in such a way that those who will live after us shall never be able to tax me with blindness to any important interest of our colony, so far as such were intrusted to my charge. But, then, the views of a professional officer should be received with that consideration, and be seconded with that support, to which they have fair claim.

I pass the subject of the incalculable value of the native woods, such as we still possess in our own forests, whether viewed in their relation to arts or as mercantile export commodities. It is a matter far too large to dwell on, even cursorily, on this occasion. Were I to enumerate all the uses already practically known of our native trees, I would have to compile a goodly volume, even were I silent on the still far ampler subject of the introduction of the thousands of different foreign trees which I should like to see here for the use of future artisans and those who are to benefit by their services. A work bearing on the nature of the forest-trees of India, by Dr. Balfour, was kindly placed in my hands by Col. Sankey, whose stay among us we at present (22d June, 1871) enjoy for advice on our water-works. Major Beddome, of Madras, issues a kindred illustrated work.

I may, however, be allowed to point to the enormous consumption of indigenous wood in some localities, as this expenditure is utterly out of all proportion to the existing supply or its present natural renovation. This question presents itself all the more gravely, as no rich coal-seams are as yet discovered, by which the fuel-supply could be augmented from short distances, at a moderate price. We have also to be cognizant that we cannot think of coal-fields as inexhaustible, even in the richest coal countries; and, although it is to be hoped that the day is very distant when the cheap results of colliery work will be marred by the much-increasing depth of the coal mines, or their partial exhaustion, yet we cannot altogether discard the idea that, so far as coals are concerned, we are working on a capital, however large it may be, without ever adding to it. In Victoria, we can neither augment the supply of burning material by peat, such as is so extensively utilized for fuel in the countries of the North, except we bring a very similar and equally useful peat from the distant and rugged heights of our Alpine mountains.

Although science has promised us prophetically other sources for applied heat—and I may add, motive power—in gases not yet within our technic reach or of universal application, we have, nevertheless, to deal with the stern realities of the day until new scientific achievements in this direction shall have been accomplished. At best, and looking ever so hopefully forward to the successes of the future, we cannot substitute in an endless array of purposes air or coal for the ever-wanted living wood, even if all that concerns climate and health could be left out of our contemplation. As an instance, then, of our present consumption, or almost immediate requirements of wood, I would like to quote one or two examples.

The able Engineer-in-chief of the Railway Department—T. Higinbotham, Esq.—has obligingly supplied me with the following data in reference to the timber at present consumed for the Government railway lines. This gentleman explains also what will most likely be needed within the next few years for this purpose.

"The number of sleepers which are used annually on the existing lines of railway, to replace decayed sleepers, is about forty thousand; and there can be no doubt that renewals at this rate at least must be continued for many years to come. Each sleeper contains three and one eighth cubic feet of timber, and for renewals Red Gum timber is used exclusively, the principal supplies being obtained from the Murray River.

"The length of fencing, which is renewed annually on the existing lines, may be taken at eighteen miles, and the quantity of timber in a mile of fencing is about three thousand cubic feet; the timber used in renewing fencing is Messmate, Peppermint, and Stringy-bark, and the durability of these timbers when used for fencing may be taken at ten years.

"There are at present nearly one hundred and twenty miles of new railway in course of construction, and sixty miles more will be undertaken before the close of this year. The new line of railway, the North-eastern, will be one hundred and eighty-one miles long, and for each mile two thousand sleepers are required, which at three and one eighth cubic feet per sleeper gives six thousand two hundred and fifty cubic feet per mile; or, for the whole length of one hundred and eighty-one miles, one million one hundred and thirty-one thousand two hundred and fifty cubic feet will be required for sleepers. The timber to be used in these sleepers will be Red Gum, Iron-bark, or Box. I have no actual experience of the durability of these timbers when used for sleepers; but I believe that it will be quite safe to reckon on their lasting for eighteen years. The ordinary Gums, when used for sleepers, will not last more than half that time.

"The quantity of timber required for fencing the North-eastern railway will be one million eighty-six thousand cubic feet. The fence-posts will be of Red Gum, Iron-bark, Blue Gum, or Box, and the rails of Stringy-bark. I think that a fence of these materials will last for eighteen years. As to projected railways, it seems to be probable that on the average from thirty to forty miles will be made for the next ten years, in addition to the North-eastern railway already in progress."

I am further told, by a gentleman conversant with our railway affairs, that the engines on the present Government line use about three thousand tons of wood a year, while about eight hundred tons more are consumed on the stations. The Government line requires one hundred and fifty thousand Blackwood keys annually. On inquiry, I have also learned that the breakwater at Williamstown will take four hundred piles, equal to eighteen thousand cubic feet, and for the superstructure of the piers ten thousand cubic feet more. The Melbourne Gas-works required, in 1870, not less than forty thousand superficial feet of Red Gum timber. The quantity of Red Gum wood required for these and other purposes cannot be increased by supplies from Tasmania, as the tree does not exist there. Again: the true Blue Gum-tree does not naturally occur beyond Victoria and Tasmania. If complete wood statistics could be collected, both of our daily requirements in town, on land, and on sea, and statistics also as to what really sound and straight timber is still available, some serious realities would be brought before us.

At Ballarat, Creswick, Beechworth, Yackandandah, Sandhurst, Heathcote, Maryborough, Avoca, Castlemaine, Fryer's Creek, and Ararat, some of the timber for the mines has to be brought already from distances as remote as ten to sixteen miles, according to returns of the Mining Surveyor, kindly furnished by Mr. R. Brough Smyth. At Pleasant Creek the miners have to go every year a mile further for their wood.

I quote the following important statement from Mr. R. B. Smyth's Mineral Statistics of Victoria for 1870:

Table showing approximately the Quantity and Cost of Timber consumed annually for Mining Purposes in the several Mining Districts, from returns made by the Mining Surveyors and Registrars.

District	Item	Quantity	£	s.	d.
BALLARAT	Firewood, etc.	320,601 tons.	203,024	4	7
	Props and cap-pieces	1,650,555 pcs.			
	Laths and slabs	4,274,798 pcs.			
	Sawn timber	5,772,110 feet.			
BEECHWORTH	Firewood, etc.	45,600 tons.	33,639	17	4
	Props and cap-pieces	155,778 pcs.			
	Laths and slabs	566,050 pcs.			
	Sawn timber	706,200 feet.			
SANDHURST	Firewood, etc.	129,750 tons.	91,551	8	4
	Props and cap-pieces	290,300 pcs.			
	Laths and slabs	1,174,500 pcs			
	Sawn lumber	614,800 feet.			
MARYBOROUGH	Firewood, etc.	98,373 tons.	53,647	4	3
	Props and cap-pieces	198,071 pcs.			
	Laths and slabs	809,182 pcs.			
	Sawn timber	786,987 feet.			
CASTLEMAINE	Firewood, etc.	68,190 tons.	29,581	14	5
	Props and cap-pieces	142,791 pcs.			
	Laths and slabs	109,143 pcs.			
	Sawn timber	456,100 feet.			
ARARAT	Firewood, etc.	91,360 tons.	23,934	0	11
	Props and cap-pieces	19,302 pcs.			
	Laths and slabs	70,021 pcs.			
	Sawn timber	250,000 feet.			
GIPPS LAND	Firewood, etc.	12,744 tons.	9,508	4	3
	Props and cap-pieces	37,656 pcs.			
	Laths and slabs	18,802 pcs.			
	Sawn timber	202,581 feet.			
	Total Cost		£444,886	14	1

As a further evidence of the imperative necessity of finding wood by a mode different to the present means of obtaining it I translate and condense a portion of a letter from an accomplished mining engineer at Clunes (Wolfgang Mueller, Esq.), a spot which once boasted of forest scenery: The fuel required for the steam-engines alone at the mines of Clunes amounts, at the present rate of working, to not less than one million three hundred and eight thousand cubic feet annually. The nearest forest is ten miles distant; the price per cord (of one hundred and twenty-eight cubic feet) is 27s. The cost of transit of the above engine-fuel amounts alone to, approximately, £10,000 pro anno; the whole expenditure being about £15,000. The round wood, for subterranean use in the mines of Clunes, now annually comes to one hundred and sixty thousand running feet, at a value of £2,400; and this round wood cannot now be obtained nearer than from twenty to twenty-five miles. The sawn and split timber for the Clunes mines has to be carried quite as far, adding about £700 to the wood expenses for these mines, the total being probably not less than £20,000 annually! No allowance is, however, made in these calculations for the domestic fuel of the miners. The price of wood is trebled already by cartage at that spot.

No natural local upgrowth, even if not destroyed by fire or traffic, I am confident can come up to this rate of consumption; and it is evident that annually the price for wood at these mining works must increase; for many mine this may become a question altogether as to the possibility of its further remunerative working. The mining operations, moreover, are generally at a yearly increase, through new gold discoveries in the district spoken of, and elsewhere. Although, on the Clunes mines, the price of wood has not materially risen during the last six years, it must be borne in mind that remuneration of labor has sunk, indicating, in reality, a considerable increase in the price of the fuel. New railway lines may, certainly, bring wood, for a time, at moderate prices, to the miners; but this measure copes not with the real difficulty of the wood question, but only defers it, as such sources of supply will also become exhausted, while carriage, from an indefinite distance, will become a financial impossibility. The present price of coal, at Clunes, is far too high to allow it to be substituted for wood. Now let us pass on to still other considerations bearing on this question. It so happens that the decrease of timber in our colonies is hastened by other agencies than those of sacrifice for utilitarian supply. Irrespective of the ordinary causes by which, in many countries, the virgin forests became devastated, there are, additionally, others which operate in our colony to augment the extensive destruction of woods. The miner ignites the underwood, with a view of uncovering any quartz-reefs or tracing mineral riches of other kinds. Although he desires only to force thus his way through a limited space of scrub, or uncover, for inspection, a small extent of ground, he really sets, sometimes, the whole forest on fire, unchaining the furies of the fiery element, which, in its ruinous and rapid progress, consumes innumerable stately trees, requiring the growth of one or even several centuries to attain their spacious dimensions. The burning trees, a prey of the flames, carry with them many others in their fall;

others become partially scorched, and linger gradually to decay; others become at least so far impaired as to offer no longer a sound or superior timber. Very aged Eucalyptus-trees are almost always suffering already from natural decay in the central portions of the stem. It is far from me to wish to impede the operations and progress of the miners, to whose intelligence and hard-working activity this country owes so much; but the advantages of gold-mining in our ranges may sometimes be too dearly bought at the expense of very extensive forest-destruction, with all the evils concomitant to it, or sure to follow it. Many other causes—such as the carelessness of travelers—set also frequently portions of the forest on fire, while the control over the devastation is lost.

The answer to remonstrances amounts usually to an opinion that more wood is springing up again than has been destroyed; but let us ask, how long will it be until the suckers, saplings, or seedlings, which, undoubtedly, in many instances, occupy the burned ground, forming perhaps impenetrable thickets, until they will really have advanced to the size of timber-trees, fit for the saw-mill? In other localities, less densely wooded, where the trees were so dispersed as to give to the natural scenery, before it was disturbed, a park-like appearance, in such localities, which impressed on many of the original Australian landscapes so much peculiarity, the growth of bushy plants becomes, as a rule, by occupation of the ground, quickly destroyed; the shelter and shade, which kept the mostly rather horizontal roots of the Eucalyptus trees cool and moist, become largely withdrawn; the pendent leaves and lax or distant ramifications of the tree itself giving but partial shade. The soil, moreover, remains no longer porous and permeable to moisture—it gets hardened, bare and consolidated by traffic and heat; the necessary moisture is wanting to keep the bark pliable, and to maintain the circulation of the sap active or normal; bark and wood are getting fissured and partly lifelesss; and now places of seclusion, as well as a wood fit for their ready attack, are given to numerous kinds of coleopterous and other insects, which, by boring the ligneous tissue, are sure to complete the destruction of the trees. Pictures of absolute misery of this kind may be noticed around our city in all directions. I have succeeded in saving many a venerable tree on the ground under my control, and in arresting the incipient decay by merely surrounding the base of the stem with earth turfed over, serving as seats; or by removing the endless quantity of mistletoe, which sucks the life-sap out of the branches, the invader perishing with its victim, there being no longer a multitude of native birds in populous localities to devour the mistle-berries. In many low localities, again, the ground, indurated by traffic, collects a superabundance of moisture, which becomes stagnant, and detrimental to the trees of such spots. Various other peculiar causes tend to the decay of our trees: to allude to all is beyond our present object.

How to provide, therefore, in time, the wood necessary for our mines, railways, buildings, fences, and as well as for the ordinary domestic and other purposes, becomes a question which from year to year presses with increased urgency on our attention, the consideration of which we have already far too long deferred. It may certainly be argued that in the eastern portion and some of the southern parts of the Victorian territory abundance of forests still exist — enough to supply all wants for many years to come. This is perfectly true in the abstract; but how does this argument apply, when we well know that such timber occurs in secluded places, mostly on high and broken ranges, without roads. And even if the latter were constructed — which certainly will be required gradually—at what price can such timber be conveyed to the required distance? Suppose, however, that all these difficulties had been overcome, whence are we to obtain the deals of northern Pines, the boards of the Red Cedar, and the almost endless kinds of other woods which future artisans will require? For, assuredly, neither Europe nor North America can sustain the heavy call on their indigenous and even planted forests for an indefinite period to come. Tropical woods might for a time be brought from the jungles of three continents, but certainly not at a small cost. Besides, tropical trees, as a rule, are not gregarious; we cannot judge beforehand, in every instance, of their durability and other qualities; we cannot recognize their extraordinary variety of sorts specifically from mere inspection of the logs, and we should find ourselves soon surrounded by endless difficulties and perplexities were we to depend on such resources alone. Would it not be far wiser timely to create independent resources of our own, for which we have really such great facility? With equal earnestness another aspect of the timber question, as concerning our national economy, forces itself on our reflection. The inhabitable space of the globe is not likely to increase, except through forces which would initiate a new organic creation, or, at all events, bring the present phase in the world's history to a close; but while the area of land does not increase, mankind, in spite of deadly plagues, of the horrors of warfare, and of unaccountable oppressions and miseries, which more extended education and the highest standard of morals can only reduce or subdue — mankind, in spite of all this, increases numerically so rapidly that before long more space must be gained for its very existence. Where can we look for the needful space? Is it in the tropic zones, with their humid heat and depressing action on our energies? Or is it in the frigid zone, which sustains but a limited number of forms of organism? Or is it rather in the temperate and particularly *our* warm temperate zone, that we have to offer the means of subsistence to our fellow-men, closely located as they in future must be? But this formation of dense and at the same time also thriving settlements, how is it to be carried out, unless, indeed, we place not merely our soil at the disposal of our coming brethren, but offer with this soil also the indispensable requisite of a vigorous industrial life, among which requisites the easy and inexpensive access to a sufficiency of wood stands well-nigh foremost.

I may be met with the reply that the singular rapidity of the growth of Australian trees is such as to bring within the scope of each generation all that is required, as far as wood is concerned; and as a corollary it would follow that each generation should take advantage of the facility thus brought locally within its reach. I can assure this audience that enlightened nations abroad do far more than this, and would not rest satisfied with the greater facilities here enjoyed; they provide, with keen forethought and high appreciation of their duty for their followers, that beforehand which cannot be called forth at any time at will. If we examine this part of the question more closely, we shall find much to think about—much to act upon. Not even all our Eucalypts are of rapid growth; they, further, belong to a tribe of trees with a hard kind of wood, which, though so valuable for a multitude of purposes, cannot supply all that the needs of life daily demand from us for our industrial work.

The quick-growing Eucalypts, among which the Blue Gum-tree of this colony and Tasmania stands pre-eminent, are comparatively few in number, nor are these few all of gigantic size. They are, moreover, restricted in their natural occurrence to limited tracts of country, from which they must be established by the hand of man in other soil for the necessities of other communities—for the gratitude of other populations. Then, again, the Pines of foreign lands, often impressing a splendor on their landscapes, must be brought to our shores—to our Alps—with an intention of utilizing every square mile of ground, however unpromising in its sterility; for, after all, that square mile represents a portion, albeit so small, of the land-surface of the globe. Look at the picture on this wall; see how the Norway Spruce (which gives us so much of our deals and tar) insinuates its massive roots through the fissures of disintegrating rocks, or, failing to penetrate the stony structure, sends its trailing roots over the surface and down the sides of the barest rocks until they have found a genial soil, however scanty, on the edge of a precipice. Nature — ever active and laborious, ever wise and beneficent — allows the tree thus to live, thus to convert the solid bowlders finally into soil, and all the time adds unceasingly to the treasures of the dominions of man. But just as time, with its measured terms in fleet course, passes irresistably onward and irrevocably away, so also have we to await the approaching time, which all our wishes cannot accelerate in its unalterable measure.

> " Onward its course the present keeps,
> Onward the constant current sweeps,
> Till life is done ;
> And did we judge of time aright,
> The past and future in their flight
> Would be as one.
>
> Let no one fondly dream again
> That hope and all her shadow-train
> Will not decay ;
> Fleeting as were the dreams of old,
> Remembered like a tale that 's told ;
> They pass away."
>
> LONGFELLOW (from "*Manrique*").

We have, therefore, to await with patience these measured terms before the child in its youthful impetuosity can reach the age of its highest hopes and supposed glory — but, alas ! leaving often a far happier phase behind ; or before a tree, from its youthful grace, can have advanced to sturdy strength or lofty height, to fulfill also its destiny and offer us its gifts. We cannot call forth age at pleasure ; at best there is involved a lapse of years before a timber-tree can yield a plank, a beam, or even as much as a solid post.

I have endeavored to arrive at some idea of the

real age of the larger trees, which are sinking daily under our axes, often sacrificed unnecessarily. On this occasion, as an apt one, I may, then, explain that a period of a quarter or even half a century must elapse before a solid plank, hardened by age, can be obtained from even a rapid-growing Eucalyptus-tree. It is estimated to require twenty to twenty-five years before even a sleeper of Blue Gum-wood can be obtained from a tree planted in ordinary soil; and that double the time will elapse before a sown tree of the still more durable Red Gum Eucalyptus will furnish sleepers, such as hitherto have been in use for our railway works. But a supply of fuel from these trees may be obtained much earlier. Mr. Adam Anderson, a timber merchant of this city, concurs in this estimate.

Yet for forest operations we enjoy here advantages of two-fold kind, for which in middle Europe we are justly envied. We can disseminate quickly-growing Eucalyptus-trees in the most arid districts; we can add to them, as a first shelter, many of the native Casuarinas and Acacias, and thus gain cover for less hardy trees of other countries. On the other hand, we find in the moist and rich valleys of our ranges a vast extent of space, where, under the mild influence of the clime, sub-tropic trees could be reared millionfold; where, for instance, whole forests of the Red Cedar might be originated. Besides, we do not stand at any disadvantage if we want to raise a belt of seacoast Pines all along the shores, or if we wish to rear the Norway Spruce, or Silver Fir, or Larch, or Weymouth Fir, or the Douglas Pine, or any of the Pitchpines of North America; because we can call forth, if we like, whole forests of them on sub-alpine heights, never yet thus utilized.

Suppose we reckon that one hundred forest-trees would be required to be planted on an acre, allowing for periodic thinning out; and assuming that for climatic and hygienic considerations, as well as for the maintenance of wood supply, we should require finally one fourth of our Victorian territory kept as a forest-area, we would expect to possess one billion five hundred and sixty-eight million trees, and to provide for their timely restoration in proportion to their removal or natural loss.

Most of us are lulled into security by seeing that we receive, as yet, our foreign woods in the course of ordinary traffic, and we are not easily inclined to think that the supply may cease suddenly, or be obtainable only at an exorbitant expense. Even in the United States of America there are places where the price of fuel and timber has already risen fourfold. We are told that recently, in the States of Wisconsin and Michigan alone, during one single year, two million of Pine-trees were cut for lumber; and it is estimated that at the present rate of destruction no timber-trees will be left in those States after fifty years, while it will take a century to replace them, if even this be possible. Quebec exported, in 1860, not less than seventy million cubic feet of squared or sawn timber, equal to about a million tons of wood — a large share yielded by the Weymouth Pine (Pinus strobus)—not taking into account the current local consumption. This tree, yielding the white American Pine-wood, requires fully sixty years of growth before it can be sawn into timber of any good size. During the first two years of the recent civil war in North America, twenty-eight thousand Walnut-trees were felled to supply one single European factory with the material for gun-stocks, demanded for this fratricidal war. Is it not right to reflect timely on the vast extensions of railroads, manufactures, mines, ship-building, dwellings, and so forth, and then to ask, Where is the wood-supply to come from? The requirements in this direction must necessarily rise with the increase of the population and the augmented refinements of civilization, yet the area of supply we see constantly decreasing. The loss on wheat crops during four of the more recent years in the State of Michigan alone, for want of shelter against cutting winds, was estimated at £5,000,000, and this is regarded as the mere sequence of the removal of the forests, and not traceable to exhaustive culture. Cereal crops and vines were destroyed in many parts of South Europe, also, through the complete want of shelter.

"More bleak to view the hills at length recede,
And less luxuriant, smoother vales extend;
Immense horizon-bounded plains succeed—
Far as the eye discerns, without an end."

BYRON.

The Commissioner of the Land Office of the United States (Report for 1868) considers the Live Oak (Quercus virens)—one of the best for ship-building—nearly exterminated for all practical purposes, at least as far as native forests are concerned; while the Walnut timber of North America, so much prized for cabinet-work, has well-nigh shared the same fate. The transit of Walnut-wood from Missouri to New York renders it already nearly as expensive as Mahogany, whereas the latter has become likewise in West India and Central America an article of great scarcity, and, therefore, this important tree should be copiously planted in the forests of tropical Australia. In the earlier part of this century the supply of Saul timber of Lower India (Shorea robusta) was thought inexhaustible; but now, already, this heavy and durable wood is hardly any longer procurable for ship-building and engineering work, for which it is so much sought. The axes of the woodmen will also soon make such an inroad into the comparatively limited Yarrah forests of West Australia that also this timber, which for salt-water works is almost incomparable, will cease to be available long before a new and sufficient supply can be raised by regular culture.

The Land Commissioner of the United States further reports, in 1868, that the frequent excessive droughts, and the occasional destructive inundations experienced a quarter of a century ago in Iowa, Kansas, and Nebraska, have much diminished since the regular settlement brought tree plantations and other cultures into the extensive treeless prairies. Iowa planted, in 1867, about seventy-six square miles of forest, and one thousand eight hundred and eighty four miles length of hedges. On the other hand, it is estimated already, in 1864, by Mr. P. T. Thomas, of New York, that the whole regions east of the Mississippi would be stripped of all really useful timber within twenty or thirty years; while even for fuel great inroads are constantly made into the American forests, coal not being everywhere accessible in the States. The Hon. T. M. Edmonds (*Report of the Department of Agriculture of U. S. for* 1868) foresees the exhaustion of the timber resources of the United States in half a century, under existing circumstances, whereas by that time the demand will be quadrupled. Mr. Simmonds calculates the importation of wood into France during 1865 at 154,000,000 francs, or about £6,000,000, the ratio of import being at an increase, notwithstanding that the forest area of that empire was reduced, within a century, to one half—namely, from one third, in the latter part of the last century—to hardly more than one sixth now. But if the population of Middle Europe consumed proportionately as much native wood as the inhabitants of the United States, then, in less than half a century, no forest whatever would be left in Europe. These conclusions are borne out by the U. S. Commissioner of Lands, the Hon. Jos. S. Wilson. In the States east of the Mississippi, six billion cubic feet of wood were consumed for timber and fuel in 1860, at a time when no war laid hand on the forests. Hence, one million of acres of forest-land must be cleared, in the Eastern States of the Union, to find the wood for a years' local requirements. The shipment of lumber, in one of the latter years, from Chicago, was one billion four hundred million cubic feet, besides two hundred and seventeen million laths, and nine hundred and twenty-eight million shingles. In 1866, the products of the California lumber trade were one hundred and ninety million of cubic feet, and thirty-eight million shingles; in 1867, about two hundred million cubic feet. Quebec exports about one million of cubic feet since a long period, annually, irrespective of home consumption. In the Pacific States exists only a supply adequate to the prospective wants of their people. The States west of the Mississippi import already timber that formerly existed in their own native forests. Likewise so in North America an enormous lot of trees is destroyed by girdling and subsequent burning, for clearing agricultural lands or pastoral runs. Thus, in the earlier part of the next century, every natural forest east of the Mississippi will have disappeared, if, with an increasing population, the same rate of consumption is going on. For the States west of the great river, in which forest-land is much less extensive, the prospects are still more alarming. Hence, Australia cannot indifferently look forward for soft-wood from these places.

To give some idea how long a time will elapse before actual timber, not merely firewood, is obtained from planted trees, I subjoin a brief list of the more common Middle European forest trees, together with notes of their age when eligible for various timber purposes:

Beech	60-110	years.
Hornbeam	70-100	"
Oak	70-120	"
Alder	30-80	"
Birch	40-70	"
Silver Fir	60-150	"
Norway Spruce	60-150	"
Scotch Fir	30-60	"
Larch	30-80	"*

That, however, in our Winterless zone, such of these trees as will endure a warmer clime would advance with more quickness to maturity must be

* It should be remembered that most of our forest ranges are naturally devoid of Pine-wood, only one species of Callitris occurring in a few limited mountain districts, while our second Callitris is a desert species. Without coniferous trees of our own we shall finally experience difficulty of obtaining the required supply of deals, pitch, turpentine, and pine-resin. Doubtless, for many wood-structures now iron is substituted, but even a ship or a house cannot be built entirely of iron, and the very production of the iron is dependent on fuel. In the absence of coal, the use of iron, involving here an expenditure for heavy freight, must necessarily be limited.

readily manifest. The accurate Customs returns for the last year show an importation of foreign woods to the value of £223,769 ; there was scarcely any export. This very month the imported building-wood sent to Sandhurst alone has cost £58,000. Some countries have not been altogether unmindful of the conservation of their forests. Germany, already much devastated at the time of the Romans, received its first forest laws as far back as the reign of Charlemagne — indeed, with the commencement of agriculture and the settling of the nomadic hunter on fixed habitations. The forests thus discontinued to be common property, and in the fourteenth century commenced already a forest economy. Full legislation, regular management and actual cultivation of trees on an extensive scale, date back one hundred and fifty years. Venice formed its forest laws already in the fifteenth century. Although the desire for ample hunting-territory gave a great impulse to the restrictions placed on the encroachment of the Middle European forests, this at the same time saved them to the country.

Within the operations of wood culture may also be included that of subduing drift-sand, and solidifying the latter finally by plantations. For this purpose can be chosen the Haleppo Pine, Cluster Pine, Scotch Fir, or our own less arboreous so-called seashore Tea-trees (Melaleuca parviflora and Leptospermum lævigatum), further the drooping She-oak (Casuarina quadrivalvis), the coast Honeysuckle (Banksia integrifolia), and also our desert cypress, or so-called Murray Pine. As not only in close vicinity to our fine city one wilderness of shifting sand exists, but as also in other places of our shores the sand is invading villages, towns, and, perhaps, harbors, and as, moreover, many a desert spot inland may be reclaimed, I would remark that, to arrest the waves of the sand, some wickerwork or cover of brush is needed on the storm side. Large seaweeds help to form such covering. Sods of Mesembryanthemum, to which the unpoetic name of "Pigfaces" is here given, and which abounds on our coast, should copiously be scattered over the sand-ridges; wild cabbage, celery, sea-kale, samphire, New Zealand spinach (Tetragonia), chamomile, and various clovers and bloom plants should be sown, and creeping sand-grass (Festuca litoralis, Triticum junceum, Buffalo-grass, Agrostis stolonifera), etc., should be planted, particulary, also, sand-sedges and sand-rushes, among the best of which are Carex arenaria, and here the Sword Rush (Lepidosperma gladiatum). Psoralea pinnata and Rhus typhinum, Prunus maritima (the Canadian sea-coast plum), Ailanthus glandulosa, proved also valuable in this respect. As eligible, I may add, also, the native couch-grass (Cynodon Dactylon), the South African Ehrharta gigantea, the European Psamma arenaria, Elymus arenarius (or Lyme), even the Live-oak (Quercus virens); as also another American Oak (Quercus obtusiloba), and the Turkey Oak (Quercus cerris), and, perhaps, Poplars, some Willows, and, among firs, the Pinus insignis, Pinus edulis, P. rigida, and P. Australis. The common Brake Fern helps also much to conquer the sand. The New Zealand flax covers coast-sand naturally, within the very exposure of the spray.* It is need-

* Dr. Jam. Hector calculated that in New Zealand an acre of good flax land contained about one hundred thousand leaves of the Phormium tenax, and yields about ten tons weight of dried leaves; or, if only the outer leaves are taken, four tons. The yield of clean fiber is about twenty-three one hundredths of the green leaf.

less to remark that exclusion of traffic from the sand is imperative, as also security against ingress of goats and domestic animals of any kind, otherwise the effort is hopeless. Fencing of the area and stringent municipal laws will make, however, any operations of this kind, even without great expense, a success, as, in consequences of my advice, has been shown at Queenscliff. Wood-culture on drift-sand carries with it also the recommendation of providing the needful belt of shelter which each coast should possess. There are a few other Pines—for instance, Pinus Taeda, the Loblolly Pine of North America, and several other trees which grow fast in sand, whenever it is no longer moving; they endure the sea-storms, gradually consolidate the soil, and render it, in course of time, arable. In South Africa, some Proteæ and Leucospermums, the Virgilia, also Myrica, grow in coast-sand. All these planting operations must be performed very early, and in the cool season. The grasses and herbs must precede the pines and other trees. Technic industries will gain from these pines in due time.

I now beg to offer some brief data in reference to the present consumption of wood in Victoria.

After the perusal of various official returns, I am inclined to assume that twenty tons would be a fair average of the quantity of fuel consumed in each household. This would amount to rather more than three millions of tons of wood as the present annual requirement of domestic fuel in this colony. In the city and suburbs the consumption is considerably less than in the farming districts, on account of the use of coal. In reference to the return of mining-wood, quoted on this occasion, a large allowance must yet be made for the enormous mass of wood from the felled trees, which is left unutilized in the ranges, the distance, in many cases, being too great to convey the off-fall of the timber for the purpose of fuel. The following data convey some information on the annual consumption of wood in various districts :

	Tons.
Ararat (under license)	13,146
" (without ")	13,146
Blackwood Mining Division	12,000
Buninyong	40,000
Colac (for saw-mills, 6,000 tons ; posts and rails, 6,000 tons ; shingles, 2,000 tons ; fuel, 30,000 tons)	44,000
Creswick (sawn timber for Clunes, 15,000 tons ; sawn timber for Amherst, 2,000 tons ; sawn timber for Creswick, 2,500 tons ; fuel for Clunes, 30,000 tons ; fuel for Creswick, 20,000 tons)	69,500
Castlemaine	37,500
Casterton	14,000
Daylesford (mining timber, 20,000 tons ; fuel, 50,000 tons)	70,000
Dunkeld—sawn timber, 800,000 feet ; rails, 20,000 pieces ; Red Gum posts, 10,000 pieces.	
Eltham	13,600
Fryerstown	57,200
Geelong	52,000
Grant	4,600
Maryborough	200,000
Nunawading (cut under license)	10,000
" (" without ")	190,000
Sandhurst	300,000
(Another informant gives the approximate quantity used solely for fuel at 160,000 tons.)	
St. Arnaud	6,500
Talbot (Shire of) and Borough of Amherst—Domestic fuel for 2,887 houses, at 6 cords or 19 1-5 tons, 55,430 tons ; mining timber, 18,368 tons ; mills, 3,200 tons ; charcoal, 3,328 tons ; public institutions, 2,560 tons ; bakers, etc., 1,600 tons ; fencing and building, 6,400 tons	90,886

Taradale (two sevenths for mining and five sevenths for fuel)	8,750
Tarnagulla.......20,000 to	30,000
Tylden (for fuel, 3,890 tons; saw-mills, 15,500 tons; for splitter's use, 2,476 tons)	21,466
Villiers, County of (approximately)	150,000
Whittlesea—As much as 1,800 trees are annually used for palings, shingles, etc.	
Winchelsea	28,600
Wood's Point	8,700
Woodend (for firewood and split or squared timber cut under license, wholly exclusive of that used by saw-mills)	41,181

On the modes of raising or renovating forests, not much can be said on this occasion. For natural upgrowth, perfect clearing and fencing is recommendable. Subsequently, the removal of young, crooked trees and the surplus of saplings is needed. Seedlings may be transferred from spots where they stand too densely, to more open or bare places. Suckers should be destroyed where the gain of good timber is an object. Periodic clearing of young trees is effected according to the rate of growth of the particular species; lopping of branches is advisable should they densely meet. For broadcast sowing, the ground should be completely cleared and burnt. By breaking the ground a great acceleration of growth of the trees is attained, even to a tenfold degree. Planting in rows affords the best access for subsequent thinning and successive removal of the timber; the Quincunx system will give approach in three directions. Pines are planted in Germany only about seven feet apart, as they require least room of all trees; but fifteen feet is a fair distance at an age of forty years. The New Hampshire Pine stands only five or six feet apart at an age of fifty years, and yet is not prevented by this crowded growth to be then one hundred feet high; the stems are then very straight, eighteen inches in diameter at the base. If Pines and Oaks are promiscuously planted, then the former, which act as nurse-trees, are moved in ten or twenty years, and the ground is left to the Oak, or any other deciduous tree, at distances at first ten or twelve feet apart, and subsequently wider still. No decayed wood is left in planted forests, as it would harbor boring insects. Pines are considered not to increase much in value after eighty years, when most of them have attained full maturity, and grow only afterward slowly. Sometimes as many as one thousand two hundred Pine-trees are set out on an acre, with a view of early utilization of a portion of the young trees. The rate of growth may be much accelerated in most trees by irrigation; hence mountain streamlets should be diverted into horizontal ditches where forests are occupying hill-sides. The best-cultivated forests of Germany are worth from three to five times as much as native woods.

For shelter plantations, intended to yield ultimately also timber and fuel to farming populations, it is recommendable to adopt the American method, according to which belts of trees are regularly planted at about quarter-mile distance; the belts, according to circumstances, to be from four to ten rods wide, and to be formed in such direction as to front the prevailing winds. These timber-belts are usually fenced. Such shelter-trees are likely to rise to thirty feet in ten years, and have proved so advantageous as to double the farm crop, while judicious management of these tree-belts will supply the wood necessary for the farm. There are one million and four hundred thousand square miles of treeless plains in the United States, which, in due course of time, will necessarily be converted, to a great extent, into agricultural areas on account of the generally excellent soil. The Locust-tree is much chosen for shelter purposes. Denuded wood-land, of poor soil, left undisturbed to natural renovation, has become, in some populous localities, five times as valuable as the adjoining inferior tillage or pasture-land. For the greatest profit in fuel, the trees, in some parts of North America, are cut about every sixteen years. We here, commanding Eucalypts, Acacias, and Casuarinas, would gain wood-harvests still speedier. The increased value of less fertile lands, through spontaneous upgrowth of timber, is estimated at sixteen hundredths of simple interest annually in woodless localities, no labor being expended on this method of wood-culture. Judicious management in thinning out enhances the value of such forest land still more. Wet and undrained grounds can be made to yield a return in Elms, Willows, Cottonwood, Swamp Cypresses, and other swamp trees, or stony declivities in Pines and Eucalypts, at a trifling cost. For details, the forest literature, which is in Germany particularly rich, should be studied. Capitalists would likely find it safer and more profitable to secure land for timber-growth than to invest in many another speculation. After the example set at Massachusetts our agricultural societies might award premiums and medals for the best timber-plantations raised in their districts. We have societies for the protection of domestic animals, native or introduced birds, young fish, etc.; why could not a strong and widely-spreading league be organized for the saving of the native forests? Might not every child in a school plant a memorial tree, to be intrusted to its care, to awaken thus an interest in objects of this kind at an early age?

Reverting to the importance of shelter, let me remark that fifty years ago the Peach flourished in North Pennsylvania, in Ohio and New York, where it cannot any longer now be grown, in consequence of the now colder and far more changeable climate, after the forests became extensively removed. Even ordinary orchards and cereal fields suffer there now. Yet, poor land will yield a better return in wood than in corn crops, and it is not too much to say that the favorable effect of a young forest on climate may be felt already, after a dozen years. Even on ordinary sheep-runs, trees are of the greatest importance, both for shelter and shade.

Having endeavored to explain forest value as it presents itself in its primary aspects — namely, in reference to its importance to Nature's great economy, and in reference to its timber resources, as viewed in the abstract — I now proceed to enter on a new field of consideration, which, though secondary in importance, is well deserving of our calm attention; and this all the more since this field of industrial enterprise remained yet almost bare or unharvested, whereas any utilization of this new ground must have, to inquiring minds, more than ordinary charm.

I therefore now proceed to explain some of the technologic features of woodlands.

A leading industry in all forests is the production

of charcoal. It may be made in mounds, caverns, or ovens. The method most frequently adopted is that in mounds or meilers, and to this I may devote a few explanatory words, as not every one in this hall may be conversant with the process; for, simple as the process does appear, it is, after all, not performable without some skill, if coal of a superior quality is to be the result. The wood is closely packed around a central post in regular form, the pieces either all horizontally, or, oftener, the lower vertically. Only such wood should be used as is unfit for timber; it must, however, be of one kind only, or of such various sorts as require the same degree of heat for being converted into a perfect coal. It must be sound and almost air-dry. A loamy sand-soil forms the best base for a mound; and this soil requires to be broken up, leveled and pressed, also dried by branchlets being burnt on the ground. The form of the mound or meiler is usually hemispherical, and support is given to this mound in the manner indicated in the sketch here presented, the outer support consisting of short logs of wood.

The inner part of the cover is formed of sods of grass, branchlets, rushes, and similar substances; over this is placed the outer portion of the cover, consisting of moist forest-soil, particularly fresh humus. The united covering must permit the vapors of the glowing meiler to escape. Shelter against wind is absolutely requisite; the operation of burning coal can therefore be well performed only in still air. The ignition commences from an opening left purposely, either at the base or, less frequently, at the summit of the structure, but either opening is closed again during the burning process. Caution is needed to prevent the expansive vapors and gases causing explosions during the glowing of the wood. To promote combustion on places where it may have been suppressed, holes are forced through the covering on the second or third day, particularly on the lee side.

A bursting forth of gases of a blueish hue indicates active burning, and under such circumstances the access given to the air must be closed, while new perforations are made in any yet inactive portion of the meiler.

Over-great activity of fire is suppressed by water applied to the covering, or by adding to the thickness of the latter. Strong sinking of the cover during the earlier burning proves more or less complete combustion of the coal, and it may then become necessary to refill hurriedly the holes with wood or coal, underclosure of all openings, and careful restoration of the cover thus temporarily removed on one spot. This refilling in large meilers may be required for five days in succession; but the more carefully the mound has been built, and the more watchfully the early glowing process has been conducted, the less necessity will arise for the troublesome and wasteful process of refilling. A final additional covering becomes frequently needful. The operation closes by the sinking of the cover, or by its being partially forced downward, and the ready coals are removable one day afterward. Partial withdrawals of coal can be effected from the lee side while the meiler is still active.

The specific gravity of charcoal stands generally in a precise proportion to the specific weight of the wood employed. Dryer wood realizes a heavier, moister wood a lighter coal. Slow combustion also renders the coal heavier than a more rapid burning process, because in the latter case more carbon is consumed for various volatile products formed from the wood. As a rule, the quantity of coal obtained is about a quarter of the weight of wood employed. Good coal has a slight metallic lustre, is firm, not friable, causing a clear sound when thrown on the ground. It must burn without flame and smoke. For trade purposes coal must be kept dry, as its absorption of humidity is considerable.* The heating power of coal as compared to wood is ascertained to be as one hundred to fifty-five or sixty. An equal volumen of wood produces less heating effect than the same space of coal. For technic operations the equable and more lasting heat, and the great power of radiation, give to charcoal its special value. Igniting wood for charcoal in caverns is wasteful, through the great access of air.

By the method of carbonizing wood in ovens, tar and other volatile products can be secured. The wood chosen for coal intended for gunpowder is chiefly that of Willows, Poplars, Alder, and Lime. It must be healthy, and is preferred from young trees. Woods which contain a good deal of hygroscopic salts—such as that of Elms, Firs, Oaks—are not adapted for the purpose. Extreme degrees of heat in producing coal for gunpowder or blasting powder should be avoided, otherwise the best wood will not serve the purpose, because the powder would be less ready to ignite. The yield of this coal is sixteen to seventeen one

*For extensive details consult von Berg's *Anleitung zum Verkohlen*; also, Muspratt's *Chemistry*.

hundredths from the wood. Local powder-mills are sure to be established here, especially as sulphur is readily obtainable from New Zealand. The increase of manufactures is also certain to augment the demand for wood and coal hereafter. For many industrial purposes charcoal is far preferable to fossil coal. Coals from various kinds of Victorian wood are placed before you.

It was my intention, while explaining the industrial resources of the forest, to show also how tar, vinegar and spirits might be obtained by heating wood in close vessels, at a temperature of three hundred to three hundred and fifty centigr., under a process called dry distillation. But I must reserve this subject for another occasion; for, however simple the procedure may be regarded, as far as the actual performance of this artisan's work is concerned, yet the chemic processes, which are active in this form of decomposition, are of the greatest complexity; they present, moreover, according to the wood employed and according to the degree of heat applied, some peculiarities, which as yet have not been fully investigated, holding out hope for the discovery of some new dyes and other educts. It will be scarcely credited by most of this audience that the paraffin, which now largely enters into the material for the candles of our households, is not only obtainable from bituminous slates, turf and fossil coal, but is also produced by the heating of wood under exclusion of air. This substance is furthermore a hydrocarbon of great purity; and its cheap preparation, along with other substances from our native wood, may possibly become a local source of immense wealth. For obtaining information on the products from heated wood, and the various apparatus employed in dry distillation, reference may be made to the great work, *Chemistry Applied to Arts and Manufactures*, by Professor Muspratt, a man of genius and industry, whose death within the last few months we had so deeply to deplore.

Presented to you here are samples of tar, acetic acid, and alcohol, from several of our more common woods ; also pieces of pine-wood, coated with eucalyptus tar, the black color, with its fine lustre, have remained unimpaired for a series of years. Our wood-tar would, for many industrial purposes, be equal in value to the best kinds of other tar, and may prove, in some respects, superior to them.

Among the undeveloped wood-resources we must not pass that referring to potash, particularly as this alkali can be obtained without sacrifice of any valuable timber, and from localities not accessible to the wood trade.

For the preparation of potash, the wood, bark, branches, and foliage are burnt in pits sunk three or four feet in the ground ; the incineration is continued till the pit is almost filled with ashes. Young branches and leaves are usually much richer in potash than the stem-wood ; hence they should not be rejected. The ashes thus obtained are placed, in tubs or casks, on straw, over a false bottom.

Cold water, in moderate quantities, is poured over the ash, and the first strong potash-liquid removed for evaporation in flat iron vessels, while the weaker fluid is used for the lixiviation of fresh ashes.

While the evaporation proceeds, fresh portions of strong liquid are added until the concentrated boiling fluid assumes a rather thick consistence.

At last, with mild heat and final constant stirring, the whole is evaporated to dryness. This dry mass represents crude potash more or less impure, according to the nature of the wood employed.

A final heating in rough furnaces is needed, to expel sulphur combinations, water, and empyreumatic substances; also, to decompose coloring principles. Thus pearlash is obtained.

Pure carbonate of potassa in crude potash varies from forty to eighty per cent. Experiments, as far as they were instituted in my laboratory, have given the following approximate result with respect to the contents of potash in some of our most common trees. The wood of our She-oaks (Casuarina suberosa and Casuarina quadrivalvis), as well as that of the Black or Silver Wattle (Acacia decurrens), is somewhat richer than wood of the British Oak, but far richer than the ordinary Pine woods.

The stems of the Victorian Blue Gum-tree (Eucalyptus globulus), and the so-called swamp Tea-tree (Melaleuca ericifolia), yield about as much Potash as European Beech.

The foliage of the Blue Gum-tree proved particularly rich in this alkali; and as it is heavy and easily collected at the saw-mills, it might be turned there to auxiliary profitable account, and, indeed, in many other spots of the ranges.

A ton of the fresh leaves and branches yielded, in two analyses, four and three quarters pounds of pure potash, equal to about double the quantity of the average kinds of pearlash. The three species of Eucalypts spontaneously occurring close around Melbourne —the Red Gum-tree (Eucalyptus rostrata); the Manna Gum-tree (Eucalyptus viminalis); the Box Gum-tree (Eucalyptus melliodora) produced nearly three pounds of pure potash, or about five pounds of pearl-ash from a ton of fresh leaves and branches; while a ton of the wood of the Red Gum-tree, in a dried state, gave nearly two pounds weight of pure carbonate of potassa, whereas the wood of the Blue Gum-tree proved still richer. A ton of the dry wood of the erect She-oak (Casuarina suberosa) furnished the large quantity of six and one half pounds of pure potash. This result is about equal to that obtainable from the European Lime-tree or Linden-tree, which again is one of the richest of all European trees in this respect.

Such indications may suffice to draw more fully the attention of forest settlers to an important but as yet latent branch of industry. For further details I refer to elaborate tables of the yield of potash in native trees, as the result from analyses made under my direction by Mr. Chr. Hoffmann — these tabulated statements being appended to my departmental report, presented to Parliament in 1869. The wholesale price of the best pearlash is about £3 for the cwt. in Melbourne.

I wish it distinctly to be understood that I do not advocate an indiscriminate sacrifice of our forest-trees for any solitary one of its products, such as the potash; because by any such procedure we would still more accelerate the reduction of our woods. On the contrary, good timber, fit for splitting or for the saw-mill, ought to be far too precious for potash or tar preparation. But branch-wood, bark, roots, crooked stems, and even foliage, might well be utilized for this industry, wherever the place is too remote to dispose of this material for fuel. The recommendation carries with it still more weight, if we remember how on many places the close growth of suckers or seedlings has to be thinned to allow of space for the new and unimpaired upgrowth of actual timber; whereas, moreover, now the remnants at places where trees have been felled, often block by impenetrable barricades the accessible lines of traffic through the forests, and are frequently the cause of the extensive conflagrations of the woods, by placing so much combustible, dry, and mostly oily material within the easy reach of the current of flames. Should, unfortunately, the fiery element have anywhere swept through the forest, it may then prove advantageous to collect the fresh ashes before they are soaked by rain, with the object of extracting thus large quantities of potash. The whole process of potash preparation being one of the simplest kind, and involving only a very trifling expense in casks and boiling-pans, can be carried out anywhere as a by-work, the profit thus being not reduced by skilled or heavy labor or by costly plant. The demand for potash must always be considerable, as it is required for the factories of niter (particularly from soda saltpeter), one of the three principal ingredients of gunpowder and blasting-powder; it is needed also for glass, alum, various kinds of soaps, dyes, and many chemicals.*

Potash, although universally distributed, is best obtained in the manner indicated. I may remark, however, though deviating from my subject, that it is one of the most potent constituents in all manures,

* Flint-glass contains about a fifth pure pearlash; crown-glass, the best window-glass, rather more than a quarter. Some potash-niter is wanted also in either case.

being especially needed in the soil for all kinds of root-crops, for vine and maize ; nor can most other plants live without it altogether, although the quantity required may be small ; but I must add, for manuring, potash by itself would be far too valuable.

Almost every kind of forage affords potash salts, these being among the necessaries for the support of herbivorous animals. Their undue diminution in food is the cause of various diseases, both in the animal and vegetable world ; or predisposes, by abnormal chemic components of the organisms, to disease.

The muscles of the human structure require a comparatively large proportion of carbonate of potassa ; it is also absolutely required in blood, predominating in the red corpuscles. Plants grown in soil of rocks containing much feldspar — such as granite, gneiss, syenite, some porphyries, diorite—are always particularly productive in potash, potassium entering largely into felspatic compounds. The latter mineral yields, in most cases, from twelve to fourteen per cent. of potassa, which, if changed to carbonate, would become augmented by nearly one half more. It is fixed chiefly to silicic acid in feldspar, and thus only tardily set free through disintegration, partly by the chemic action of air, water, and various salts, partly through the mechanic force of vegetation.* The importation of potash into Victoria during 1870 was only one hundred and seventy tons, but, with the increase of chemic factories, we shall require much more.

It has justly been argued that the chemic analysis affords a very unsafe guidance to the artisan, as regards the quantity of potash obtainable from any kind

* The proverb of chemistry — " *Corpora non agunt, nisi fluida* " — is here also applicable.

of tree or other plant, inasmuch as necessarily the percentage must fluctuate according to the nature of the soil, this, again, depending on geologic structure and the quality and quantity of decaying foliage on any particular spot. It should, however, not be quite forgotten that most plants have a predilection for that soil which contains, in regions otherwise favorable to them, also due proportions of such mineral particles as are essentially necessary for the normal nutrition of the peculiar species; for, otherwise, in the wild combat for space it would succumb or cede before the more legitimate occupant of such soil. Hence, at a glance, even from long distances, we may recognize in many of our forest regions an almost abrupt line of demarcation between the gregarious trees, where one geologic formation meets or replaces the other. Thus, trees richer in potash, or oils, or any other product, may often be traced with ease over their geologic area, for which purpose the admirable maps of Mr. Selwyn and his collaborators afford us here in Victoria also in this respect already so very much facility.

I have often been led to think that many an indigent person might find employment by collecting the wood-ashes, which, as a powerful manure, or as material for a local potash-factory, ought to realize a fair price. Such an employment would be probably as lucrative as collecting glass, or bones, or substances for paper-mills, while the ashes, now largely wasted, would be fully utilized.

It may be assumed that, at an average, the ash of our ordinary Eucalypts contains ten per cent. of crude potash, equal to about five per cent. pure potash. A bucketful of wood-ash, such as we daily remove from our domestic fire-places, contains about twenty-five pounds, from which, accordingly, about two and one half pounds of inferior, or one and one fourth pounds of superior potash, may be obtained; the former being worth about sixpence per pound, the latter double the price. For ascertaining the contents of carbonate of potassa in crude potash or pearlash, certain instruments, well known as alkali-meters, are constructed. The heaviest ashes, as a rule, contain the greatest proportion of potash. The brake-fern, so common on many river-banks and sandy tracts of the country, is rich in this alkali.

Apart from my subject, I may, however, say that there are other sources of potash-salts than trees alone. Chloride of potassium is obtained from some large salt-beds, for instance, in Prussia. From this source it was supplied to British manufactories, in 1869, to the extent of one hundred and fifty-four thousand four hundred and sixty-eight hundred weight, valued at above £60,000. This chloride is besides obtained, under Mons. Balard's process (Report of Juries at the International Exhibition for 1862), in considerable quantities from sea-water, as one of the contents to be utilized. From this chloride the various potash salts, otherwise largely obtained from pearlash, can be also prepared. Chlorides and sulphates, if they occur in crude potash, can, in the process of purification, almost completely be removed through crystallization from the greatly concentrated solution.

Let us now approach another forest industry, one quite unique and peculiar to Australia—namely, the distillation of volatile oil from Eucalyptus and allied

Myrtaceous trees. While charcoal, tar, wood-vinegar, wood-spirit, tannic substances and potash, are obtainable and obtained from the woods of any country, we have in Australia a resource of our own in the Eucalyptus oil. In no other part of the globe do we find the Myrtaceæ to prevail; in Europe it is only the Myrtus of the ancients, the beautiful bush for bridal wreaths, which there represents this particular family of plants; and although copious species of Eugenia and other berry-bearing genera, including the aromatic clove and allspice, are scattered through the warmer regions of Asia, Africa, and America, all pervaded by essential oil, they do not constitute the main bulk of any forests as here, nor can their oil in chemic or technic properties be compared to that of the almost exclusively Australian Eucalyptus. This special industry of ours exemplifies also, in a manner quite remarkable, how from apparently insignificant experiments may arise results far beyond original anticipations. When, in 1854, as one of the commissioners for the Victorian Industrial Exhibition, held in anticipation of the first Paris Exhibition, I induced my friend, Mr. Joseph Bosisto, J. P., to distil the oil of one of our Eucalypts, I merely wished to show that this particular oil might be substituted for the comparatively costly oil of cajuput, obtained in some parts of India, and rather extensively used in some countries for medical purposes. For the exhibition of 1862 about thirty different oils were prepared by the same gentleman, chiefly from various Eucalypts, and from material mostly selected by myself for the purpose. This led not merely to determining the percentage of yield, but also to extensive experiments, here chiefly by Messrs. Bosisto and Osborne, and in London by Dr. Gladstone, in reference to the illuminating power, the solvent properties, and other special qualities of each of these oils. The principal results of these experiments were recorded in reports of the exhibition jurors at the time. Mr. Bosisto, with great sagacity and a commendable perseverance, but also at first with much sacrifice of capital, carried his researches so far as to give to them great utilitarian value and mercantile dimensions; moreover, he patented a process by which he was enabled to derive from the eucalyptus foliage the greatest amount of the purest essential oil with the least consumption of fuel and application of labor. Under this process it became possible to produce the oil at a price so cheap as to allow the article to be used in various branches of art—for instance, in the manufacture of scented soap, it having been ascertained that this oil surpassed any other in value for diluting the oils of roses, of orange flowers, and other very costly oils, for which purposes it proved far more valuable than the oil of rosemary and other ethereal oils hitherto used. Suddenly, then, such a demand arose that our thoughtful and enterprising fellow-citizen could export already about nine thousand pounds to England and three thousand pounds to foreign ports, though even now this oil is as yet but very imperfectly known abroad. The average quantity now produced at his establishment, for export, is seven hundred pounds per month. Alcoholic extracts of the febrifugal foliage of Eucalyptus globulus and Eucalyptus amygdalina have also been exported in quantity by the same gentleman to England, Germany, and America.

Similar substances from various melaleucas might be added. Originally, an opinion was entertained that all the eucalyptus oils have great resemblance to each other; such, however, proved not to be the case when it came to accurate experimental tests. Thus, for instance, the oil which in such rich percentage is obtained from Eucalyptus amygdalina, though excellent for diluting the most delicate essential oils, is of far less value as a solvent for resins in the fabrication of select varnishes. For this latter purpose the oil of one of the dwarf Eucalypts forming the Mallee Scrub, a species to which I gave, on account of its abundance of oil, the name "Eucalyptus oleosa" nearly a quarter of a century ago, proved far the best. It is this Mallee oil which now is coming into extensive adaptations for dissolving amber, Kauri resin, and various kinds of copal. Mr. Bosisto's researches are recorded in the volume of the Royal Society of Victoria for 1863; Mr. Osborne's in the Jurors' Reports of the Exhibition of 1862. For alluding so far to this oil distillation I have a special object in view. I wish to see it adopted near and far as a collateral forest industry, now that the way for the ready sale of this product is so far paved. The patentee is willing to license any person to adopt his process, and he is also ready to purchase the oil at a price which will prove remunerative to the producer. If it is now considered how inexhaustible a material for this oil industry is everywhere accessible in our ranges, how readily it is obtainable, particularly at saw-mills and at splitters' establishments, and how easily the process of the distillation can be performed, it would be really surprising should these facilities not be seized upon, and should under such favorable circumstances not a far larger export of this mercantile commodity be called forth. Those Eucalypts are the most productive of oil in their foliage which have the largest number of pellucid dots in their leaves; this is easily ascertained by viewing the leaves by transmitted light, when the transparent oil-glands will become apparent, even without the use of a magnifying lens. Mr. Bosisto is also a purchaser of scented flowers, indigenous as well as cultivated, including even the wattle flowers, for the extraction of delicate scents, under a clever process discovered by himself; and it is astonishing what an enormous demand for these perfumes exists in European markets. This may be a hint to any one living in or near the forests, where the extraction of the scent could be locally accomplished from unlimited resources, with little trouble and cost.

There exists another special industry in its incipient state among us, which might be regarded as essentially Australian, and which also might be widely extended: I mean the gathering of seeds of many kinds of Eucalyptus, and also of some Acacias and Casuarinas, for commercial export. No doubt the collecting of seeds is effected among the forest-trees of any country, and very important branches of industry these gatherings are, in very many localities abroad. But what gives to our own export trade of forest seeds such significance is the fact that we offer thereby means of raising woods with far more celerity and ease than would be possible through dissemination of trees from any other part of the globe, it being understood that the operations are instituted in climatic zones similar to our own. Trees with softer kinds of woods, such as Poplars and Willows, even though they may rival some of the Eucalypts in quickness of growth, cannot be well drawn into comparison, as most of them do not live in dry soil, nor attain longevity, nor assume gigantic dimensions, nor furnish timber of durability. But there are still other reasons which have drawn our Eucalypts into extensive cultural use elsewhere — for instance, in Algeria, Spain, Portugal, Italy, the south of France, Greece, Egypt, Palestine, various uplands of India, the savannahs of North America, the llanas of South America, at Natal and other places in South Africa, and even as near as New Zealand.* One of the advantages offered is the extraordinary facility and quickness with which the seeds are raised, scarcely any care being requisite in nursery works; a seedling, moreover, being within a year, or even less time, fit for final transplantation. Another advantage consists in the ease with which the transit can be effected, in consequence of the minuteness of most kinds of Eucalyptus seeds,† there being, besides, no difficulty in packing on account of the natural dryness of these seeds. For curiosity's sake I had an ounce of the seed of several species counted, with the following results:—

Blue Gum-tree, one ounce—sifted fertile seed grains....	10,112
Stringy-bark tree (unsifted)	21,080
Swamp Gum-tree (unsifted)...........................	23,264
Peppermint Eucalypt (unsifted)........................	17,600

* The seeds of Eucalyptus rostrata (our Red Gum-tree) are available for all tropic countries, inasmuch as this species, which is almost incomparably valuable for its lasting wood, ranges naturally right through the hot zone of Australia.

† The seeds of the West Australian Red Gum-tree (Eucalyptus calophylla) and the East Australian Bloodwood-tree (Eucalyptus corymbosa) are comparatively large and heavy.

According to this calculation we could raise from one pound of seeds of the Blue Gum-tree one hundred and sixty-one thousand seven hundred and ninety-two plants. Let us suppose, for argument's sake, that only half the seeds of such grew, the number of seedlings would be enormous; and even if only the seedlings of one quarter of the seeds of one pound finally were established, they would suffice, in the instance of the Blue Gum-tree, to cover four hundred and four acres, assuming that we planted at the rate of one hundred trees to the acre (allowing for thinning out). The following notes, for comparison, may be of interest:

One ounce of:	Contains Grains.
Pinus pinaster	730
Pinus pinea	38
Pinus haleppensis	940
Pinus alba	10,080
Cupressus sempervirens	4,970
Fraxinus ornus	316
Betula alba	34,560
Acer pseudoplatanus	183

It seems marvellous that trees of such colossal dimensions, counting among the most gigantic of the globe, should arise from a seed-grain so extremely minute.

The exportation of Eucalyptus-seeds has already assumed some magnitude. Our monthly mails conveyed occasionally quantities to the value of over £100; the total export during the past twelve years must have reached several or, perhaps, many thousand pounds sterling. For the initiation of this new resource, by his extensive correspondence abroad, the writer can lay much claim; and he believes that almost any quantity of Eucalyptus-seeds could be sold in markets

6

of London, Paris, Calcutta, San Francisco, Buenos Ayres, Valparaiso and elsewhere, as it will be long before a sufficient local supply can be secured abroad from cultivated trees.

Monsieur Prosper Ramel, of Paris, stands foremost among those who promoted Eucalyptus culture in South Europe.

Facts, such as just alluded to, may give an idea with what ease the Eucalyptus can be disseminated over extensive areas. Although the first cost of seeds, or the facilities for their transit, preservation, and germination, can only enter to a small extent into consideration, when an object so important as that of raising or restoring forests is to be attained, yet the data thus far given in reference to some of the best Eucalypts cannot but tend toward encouragement of culture here and abroad. Indeed, among nearly all the trees of the globe, most of our Eucalypts, together with species of the allied genera — tristania, angophora, melaleuca and metrosideros — produce seeds the most minute and the most copious. The seeds of the Birches, and of most species of ficus are, however, also remarkably light and numerous.

At saw-mills and splitters' establishments, the gathering of seeds, particularly through the aid of children, might be carried on most conveniently and most inexpensively, the sums realized therefrom being clear gain. The same may be said of collecting the abundant gum-resins of various Eucalypts, which, for medicinal and technologic purposes, are now in much demand for export. Purchasers in the city offer about one shilling per pound. The liquid (very astringent) exudations of the Eucalypts are also salable. The precise quantity of tannic substance to be obtained from saplings and foliage of various Eucalypts, acaciæ and casuarinæ remains yet unascertained; but it is likely large enough to base on their yield of tannic acid special forest industries.

For belts of shelter-plantations, again, no country in the warm temperate or subtropic zone could choose trees of easier growth, greater resistance, rapidity of increment, early and copious seeding, contentedness with poor soil, and yet valuable wood for various purposes, than some of the Australian acaciæ and casuarinæ. They exceed much in quickness of growth the coast shelter-pines of South Europe, Pinus haleppensis and Pinus pinaster, but are not all equally lasting. The trade in seeds of this kind is also not unimportant, and the sources of it are, at least partly, in our sylvan land.

Still another forest industry might be viewed as especially Australian, namely, the supply of Fern-trees for commercial exportation. Though about one hundred and fifty kinds of Fern-trees are now known, they are mostly children of tropical or subtropical countries, and these, again, nearly all restricted to the humid jungles or the shady valleys meandered by forest brooks. Very few species of these noble plants extend to a zone so cool as that of Victoria, Tasmania, and New Zealand. Again, among this very limited number, the stout and large Dicksonia antartica is not only one of the tallest of all the Fern-trees of the globe, but certainly also the most hardy, and the one which best of all endures a transit through great distances. Indeed, a fresh, frondless stem, even if weighing nearly half a ton, requires only to be placed, without any packing, in the hold of a vessel as ordinary goods, to secure the safe arrival in Europe,* the vitality being fully thus retained for several months, particularly if the stem is occasionally moistened, and kept free from the attacks of any animals. Through my unaided exertions these hardy Fern-trees became, like many other of our resources, fully known in many countries; and, while their value became established, a market for them has now been gained. I would, however, not countenance the vandalism of denuding every one of our Fern-glens of its pride, as, even with all care, in half a century the pristine grandeur of the scenery could not be restored; yet, when we consider that hundreds of gullies are teeming with these magnificent plants, we can well afford to render them accessible also to all the conservatories of the winterly north, in order that the inhabitants there may indulge in admiration of such superb forms of vegetable life, even though a Fern-tree group in a glass house can convey but a very inadequate idea of the wild splendor of our Fern ravines. Not without pain I have seen constructed the base of whole tramway lines in some of our forest-gullies, almost exclusively of Fern-trees, for the conveyance of timber. A watchful Forest Board would prevent such sacrifice, and would save also the tall Palm-trees of East Gipps Land from sharing the fate of those princely trees at Illawarra and elsewhere. [Since writing this, our Livistonas or Fan-palms have been protected by Government interdiction; the law forbids also the indiscriminate removal of Red Gum-trees from the banks of the Murray River. In Queensland, every bunya-

* No Fern-tree is indigenous to Europe.

bunya tree and native nut-tree is secured against being felled. The very local and circumscribed Kauri forests, known only in two limited spots, would also need some protection.] To the facilities of exporting the huge, square Todea Ferns—a commerce initiated by myself—I alluded on a former occasion.

Having dwelt on some of the technologic or mercantile products obtainable from the native forests—few, it is true—I now pass on to some brief observations in reference to enriching the resources of our woods.

Among new industries which, by introduction from abroad, are likely to be pursued in sylvan localities, that of the cultivation of the Tea shrub of China and Assam stands, perhaps, foremost. It is a singular fact that even in the genial clime of Southern Europe, and under advantages of inexpensive labor, the important and lucrative branch of Tea-culture has received as yet no attention whatever. This is probably owing to the circumstance that hitherto the laborious manual process of curling the fresh Tea-leaves under moderate heat has never yet been superseded by adopting for the purpose rollers worked and heated by steam, though such contrivance was suggested here by me many years ago.

The tea thus obtained could always be brought to its best aroma by such a mode of exact control over the degree and duration of the heat. Tea-culture in the ranges would show us which soil, or which geologic formation, produced here the best leaves. The yield of the latter would, in the equable air of the humid air of the forest-glens, be far more copious than the harvests which we obtain from the tea-bushes planted in poor soil or exposed localities near the metropolis, while localities in the ranges are often not accessible to ordinary cereal culture. But I do not speak of Tea cultivation as an ordinary field industry, but rather as a collateral occupation in forest-culture of the lower ranges.

Foreseeing the likelihood that this branch of rural culture would be adopted in many favorable warm spots of this colony, I have distributed, during the past dozen years, the Tea-bush rather extensively among country residents, partly with the view of directing attention to a plant which, even for the sake of ornamental value, is so eligible and easily grown; partly with an intention of seeing thus independent local supplies of seed forthcoming. In the same way the Cork Oak was very generally distributed by myself, in order that their acorns might, in due time, become locally accessible in very many places.

The tea, in its commercial form, will however, here, not likely be manufactured by the grower. It is more probable that whenever plantations are formed in any forest region, an enterprising man will establish amidst the tea-farms a factory for preparing the tea-leaves, and purchase the latter from the producers. This is the system by which, in many parts of South Europe, the multitude of small lots of silk-cocoons pass into the central reeling establishments; and this is the manner in which, from numerous peasants, the beet-root is obtained for the supply of sugar factories. In the same way the branches of the Sumach, a shrub which, with care, could be reared in our ranges, would be rendered saleable at a central sumach mill.* The demand for tea being so enormous, and geographic latitudes like ours being those which allow of its growth, it will be fully apparent that it must assume a prominent part in our future rural economy, particularly as the return for capital and labor thus invested and expended will be quite as early as that from the vine. The importation of tea into Victoria, during 1870, has been valued in the customs returns at £496,623; whereas Victoria might largely export this highly important and remunerative commodity.

The simple process of gathering the leaves might be performed by children.

In the foregoing pages I alluded cursorily to the Cork Oak; let me add my opinion, that in any locality with natural boundaries, such as abrupt sides of ranges, deep water-courses, where fences could be largely obviated, the Cork-tree might well be planted as a forest-tree, and thus estates be established at little cost, with hardly any expense of maintenance, from which a periodic yield of cork might be obtained for several successive generations. The investment of a limited capital for raising a cork-forest in any naturally-defined locality would, as I said, create a rich possession for bequest. Even if by new inventions an artificial substitute for cork was found, the wood of the Cork Oak would still be of some value. The State might also reserve any forest area with natural boundaries for its various wood requirements.

---

*An essay by Professor Inzenga, on Sumach-culture in Sicily, translated by Colonel H. Yule, C. B., is published in the Transactions of the Botanic Society of Edinburgh, vol. ix., 341–355, and was, on my suggestion, transferred to a local journal.

Many other cultural resources of forests are as yet very inadequately recognized. The dye-saffron might be grown as much for amusement as for the sake of its pretty flowers, just as an ordinary bulb, wherever juvenile gatherers can be had. Equally lucrative might be made the culture of another plant, the medicinal colchicum, a gay Autumnal flowering bulb worthy of a place in any garden. In apt forest spots both would become naturalized. Amidst the forests, in the glens which skirt the very base of alpine mountains, on the M'Allister River, opium was produced without any toil, almost as a play-work, to the value of £30, from an acre. Mr. Bosisto, who, on that particular locality, called forth this industry, found on analysis that the Gipps Land opium proved one of the most powerful on record, ten one hundredths of morphia being its yield. Small samples of opium prepared in the Melbourne Botanic Garden were exhibited some years ago at the International Exhibition. The Hon. John Hood, of this city, promoted much the opium industry in this country by the extensive distribution of seeds of the Smyrna poppy ; he found the yield here, in favorable seasons and by careful operation, to be from forty to fifty pounds on an acre, worth at present thirty to thirty-five shillings per pound. The value of the opium imported into Victoria during 1870, according to customs returns, was £150,681. The banks of many a forest brook, and the slopes within reach of irrigation from springs, might, doubtless, in numerous instances, be converted into profitable hop-fields, the yield of hops in Gipps Land having proved very rich. Mr. A. M. M'Leod obtained, in one instance, fifteen hundred pounds of hops from an acre of ground at Bairnsdale,

Messrs. A. W. Howitt, F. Webb, and D. Ballentine had there also large returns from their hop-fields. As an instance how large a revenue might be realized from forest land in various ways, quite irrespective of wood supply, I adduce the fact that the income obtained by the Forest Department of Hanover from the mere gathering of fruit—chiefly bleeberries—amounted to £21,750 during one of the late years. The Hanoverian forests comprise an area equal to the county of Bourke, our metropolitan county, and occupy one seventh of the territory. Speaking of Hanover, let me add, that the laws promulgated this year in that country render it compulsory on each district to line its roads with trees, the widest distance allowed from tree to tree being thirty feet; similar laws were in force long since in other parts of Germany; fruit-trees are among the trees chosen for these lines. Would it not therefore be advisable to naturalize along our forest brooks and in our shady vales such plants as the raspberry-bush, strawberry-plant, and others, which readily establish themselves? In one of my exploring tours, when it fell to my lot to discover the remotest sources and tributaries of the River Yarra, and to ascend first of all Mount Baw Baw, I scattered the seeds of the large-fruited Canada blackberry along the alpine springs; and I have since learned that this delicious fruit is now established on the rivulets of that mountain. We may hear of equal successes of experiments which I elsewhere instituted. The truffle, though not an article of necessity, might be naturalized in many of our forests, especially in soil somewhat calcareous. Would any one imagine that during one recent year (1867) the quantity collected in France was valued at £1,-

400,000 (35,000,000 francs) ? The time allotted to my address is not sufficient to add much to these instances.

On various occasions I drew attention to the likelihood of Peru-bark plants being eligible for culture in the sheltered and warmer parts of our woods, inasmuch as in brush shades of the Botanic Gardens the cinchonæ endured a temperature two or three degrees under the freezing point. Last year Cinchona-plants given by me to Mr. G. W. Robinson, of Hillesley, near Berwick, for experiment, passed quite well through the cool season without any cover. The lowest temperature at Harmony Valley, Blackwood Gully, in the Dandenong Ranges, observed during 1866 by Mr. Jabez Richardson, who, on my request, kindly undertook the thermometer readings there during that year, was still one degree above the freezing point, while the temperature at the Melbourne Observatory sunk to twenty-eight degrees Fahrenheit. Let me note, however, that simultaneously frost occurred in the open flats of Dandenong ; hence the great importance of forest shelter in cases like this. East Gipps Land, with its mild temperature, is likely to prove the aptest part of the Victorian colony for Peru-bark cultivation. Who does not remember the deep grief into which a small insular colony sunk within the last few years, when its population became actually decimated by fever, and when, after one hundred and fifty years of existence of that unhappy colony, only just the first Cinchonas had been planted.

In some of the uplands of New South Wales, where it was desirable to clear away bush vegetation—such, for instance, in which Daviesias, or native hop, predominated — angoras proved very effectual for the purpose. Doubtless there are many forest tracts where this measure could be adopted with advantage to gain grass pasture, without any injury being done to large native trees; but the smaller trees are likely to suffer, while the underwood might in many instances be better utilized for potash or oil. At all events, goats are, among pastoral animals, the most destructive to vegetation, and much of the forests on the Alps of Switzerland and Tyrol were destroyed by the indiscriminate access given to goats. The Angora, with its precious fleece, can therefore be located only in some forest regions; it thrives, moreover, in the desert.

I might allude, on this occasion, also to the great productiveness of bees in our forests, the flowers of so many of our native plants, and among them those of the Eucalypts, being mellaginous—blossoms of some kind or the other being available all the year round. Cuba, with an area less than half that of Victoria, exported, in the year 1849, so large a quantity of honey as two millions and eight hundred thousand pounds, and about one million pounds of wax. I believe the export has since increased. A forest inhabitant might devote a plot of ground near his dwelling to the earth-nut or pea-nut, an originally Brazilian plant, of which latterly about nine hundred thousand bushels were produced annually in the United States for the sake of its excellent table-oil. In *Harper's Magazine* of 1870 it is stated that of the earth-nut, in 1869, not less than two hundred and thirty-five thousand bushels were brought to New York. It is estimated that Virginia, Tennessee, Georgia, and Carolina have conjointly sent over one million bushels to market in 1870. The yield, it is said, is from eighty to one hundred and twenty bushels on an acre. The seeds are slightly roasted for the table, or pressed for a palatable oil. As much as ten shillings to twelve shillings is paid for the bushel in New York. The plant seems well eligible for forest-farms, particularly in a somewhat calcareous soil. In the garden under my control I have reared it with ease.

I intended to have spoken of the various implements especially designed for wood-culture; but time will not admit of it. Thus, merely by way of example, I place before you one of those utensils — the hohlborer, or, as it might be called, the "bore-spade" —brought into use nearly fifty years ago by a scientific forester, Dr. Heyer, of Giessen. Several thousand plants of the Scotch Fir and of other pines can be lifted with this bore-spade in a day by one forest laborer, the object being that each seedling should retain a small earth-ball, to facilitate the success of the moving process. About ten thousand such seedlings are conveyed at a time in a forest wagon.*

And yet, it must be confessed, our colony, with others in the Australian group, has accomplished but very little in any branch of sylvan maintenance, or forest culture, or the advance of industrial pursuits in our woodlands.

One precursory step, however, has been made, and this is likely to be followed. I allude to the extensive gratuitous distribution of plants to public grounds in most parts of our colony—a distribution which has been in operation under the authority of Government

* Since this lecture was delivered a short account of the bore-spade has appeared in the Melbourne *Economist*.

from ground under my control for the last twelve years. I should think it not unlikely that this raising of trees in masses will soon become also a special object of attention to the railway department, within its own areas, to re-supply its own wants.

While a divine may withdraw some of his slender means, or a teacher may devote a share of his scanty earning, to inclose the ground of his dwelling, with a view of protecting a few trees on spots not really their own, we may be sure that the authorities do not wish to see hundreds of miles of railway fences long left unutilized, so far as planting of trees is concerned, particularly as such fences for this purpose afford much ready inducement. The average width of the railway area is two and a half chains, both on the Ballarat and Echuca lines, therefore far wider than that of European lines, and spacious enough for tree plantations, at least of some kinds. The length of the N. E. Railway line will be one hundred and eighty-five miles, giving, consequently, three hundred and seventy miles' length for plantations. The slower-growing or less-lofty trees would there be on their place, such as our Red Gum-tree, the Iron-bark-tree, the W. A. Yarrah, the Blackwood-tree, the British Oak, the Quebec and Live Oak, the Cork Oak, the Elm, the Ash, the Totara, the Chestnut-tree, the Walnut, the Hickory, and many others which do not suffer from exposure; for while the railway loan will last for an indefinite period, the railway material, such as the fences, sleepers, cars, will not last forever, and for these the wood might thus inexpensively become re-available in due time. Even where the railway space is narrow the operation of lopping the planted trees along its lines might most readily be resorted to, and dangerous encroachments thereby be avoided.

No one ever expected our most serviceable Railway Department to be burdened with the additional heavy task of entering on cultural pursuits, and I see no way of attaining the object here specially indicated unless purposely financial means and administrative organizations were provided by the State.

In a special work (*Die Bepflanzung der Eisenbahn Damme*, etc., by E. Lucas, second edition, 1870) the methods adopted in Germany for utilizing the railway dams, and the free space within railway fences, for wood and fruit culture, is amply discussed. With the increasing value of culture-land this question of utilizing the spare ground along railways becomes more and more important. Where the space proves too narrow for rearing timber-trees, Hazel, Olives, Figs, Mulberries, Almonds, Osiers, Sumach, Myall, Ricinus, Blackberries, and such other lower trees or bushes as require no great attention, could doubtless be grown with profit. It might also be possible to establish advantageously permanent hedges of Hawthorn, Opuntias, Osage Orange, and other not readily-inflammable and easily-managed bushes. Luzern and Sainfoin are much cultivated along continental railway-lines as fodder-herbs.

In North America six hundred and fifty Walnuts or Hickories are planted on an acre; though standing so close, they are worth twelve shillings in twenty years for a variety of purposes. If wanted for heavy timber or nuts, they are thinned out so as to keep them twenty feet apart. This may serve as an indication how spare places on railways might be utilized. Our regular and quick communication with California is giving now easy opportunity for importing nuts of the various American Hickories and Walnut-trees in quantity; while of the ordinary Persian Walnut-tree seeds can already be obtained both here and in Tasmania. Resinous Pine-trees may possibly increase any danger of conflagrations on railway-lines. Nurseries for sowing seeds of hardy utilitarian trees might at once be established on all the railway-stations at comparatively little cost.

The only effective public effort hitherto made to anticipate the necessities of forest culture consists in the planting of public reserves, parks, church-yards, school-grounds, cemeteries, and the area of many of our public buildings. The trading horticulturists have also largely aided in the importation and raising of foreign trees.

In this effort, as already remarked, I took a prominent share, or perhaps, in many instances, it originated from impulses or supports given by myself.

Undoubtedly, it was a primary object to cover the dismal barrenness of public grounds, to help in mitigating thereby local dryness and heat, to afford shade and shelter, and to render many a barren spot a pleasing retreat.

But this was not my only object. I had a second, and, to my mind, higher one in view.

I wished that, locally, many nuclei for forest culture should be formed; that, within comparatively few years, seeds should almost everywhere become available in masses from local tree-plantations; and that thus efforts now made for parks and pleasure-grounds should be enlarged for creating more or less extensive forests.

These ideas may, perhaps, excite some surprise, yet I feel confident that they will and must be acted on before, in frightful truthfulness, the terrors of a woodless country in *our* zone, and settled with a future *dense* population, will be encountered.

Should, however, my warnings fail to impress the public mind, then at least I have placed my views on record, and should not be held responsible for interests, however vital, which the trust of my position must largely bring under my reflection and care.

My effort in supplying merely material for raising local plantations all over the colony is, however, but the first step in a great national work of progress; and I think we may reflect, not without some pride, that this public step was made in Australia here first of all.

Half a million of plants distributed by me to public institutions is, after all, but a trifle in a country that requires hundreds of millions of foreign trees, if it really is to advance to greatness and the highest prosperity; a greatness that will be retarded in the same degree as attention to this, one of its most urgent interests, is deferred.

The gifts of plants from the establishment under my control have provided the country with many a species that otherwise would not have existed here yet. Many of the magnificent or quick-growing Himalayan and California Pines, not to speak of others, became through my hand first dispersed by thousands and thousands; and although I may have incurred the displeasure of a few of the less thoughtful of my fellow-citizens, who wished the slender means of my young establishments appropriated for the ephemeral glory of floral displays, and who wished to sacrifice lasting progress to unproductive gaiety, yet I feel assured that the fair feelings of the inhabitants of Victoria in general will approve of the path of predominant utility which I struck out for myself, and will respect the considerations which prompted me, in an equitable spirit toward town and country, to attend in the first instance to pressing necessities, leaving the unnecessary or less useful for the exertions of a later time.

If a census of the trees, which are to furnish us much seed for forest culture, could be held all over the colony, perhaps my early efforts would be viewed with more justice and gratitude.

> " They did of solace treat,
> And bathe in pleasure of the joyous shade,
> Which shielded them against the broiling heat,
> And with green bough decked the gloomy glade."
>
> SPENSER.

In passing through a demolished forest, how saddening to us its aspect! What mind, capable of higher feelings, can suppress its sympathy, when we see stretched and withering on the ground a princely tree which but a few hours previously was an object of our admiration and a living monument of magnificence and glory. Do you think it had its enjoyment? Does it send mere automatically, without animation or sensibility of any kind, its crown to the sunny sky, or drink joyless the pearly dew? Do you think it closes its flowers but mechanically, or unfolds them again to imbibe light and genial warmth, absolutely without gladness or pleasure of any kind? What is vitality, and what mortal will measure the share of delight enjoyed by any organism! Why should even the life of a plant be expended cruelly and wastefully, especially if, perhaps, this very plant stood already in youthful elegance, while yet the diprotodon (a wombat of the size of a buffalo) was roaming over the forest ridges encircling Port Phillip Bay—when those forest ridges on the very place of this city were still clothed in their full natal garb. Do not assume that I lean to transmutation doctrines; or that to my understanding there is an uninterrupted transit from the thoughts which inspire the mind to the faculties of animals and to the vitality of plants! Yet that individual life, whatever it may be, which we often so thoughtlessly and so ruthlessly destroy, but which we never can restore, should be respected. Is it not as if the sinking tree was speaking imploringly to us, and when falling wished to convey to us its sadness and its grief? Like the nomadic wanderer of the Australian soil passed away before us, so I fear most of the traces of our beautiful and evergreen forest will be lost ere long.

> . . . "It is a goodly sight to see
> What heaven has done for this delicious land;
> What flowers of fragrance blush on every tree,
> What glad'ning prospects o'er the hills expand!
> But man would mar them with an impious hand."
>
> BYRON.

Beyond the plain utilitarian purposes of our forests (some of which I endeavored briefly to explain), and beyond all, the important functions which the woods have to perform in the great economy of Nature, they possess still other claims on our consideration, such as ought to evoke some feeling of piety toward them.

It was in the forests where the poetic mind of Schiller, during his early boyhood,* first of all awoke to its deep love for nature; where his strong sense for noble rectitude was formed; where he framed his ideals of all that is elevated and great. This influence of nature we see reflected in other lofty minds; it leads true genius on its luminous path. Contrast the magnificence of a dense forest, before the destructive hand of man defaced it, with the cheerless aspect of wide landscapes devoid of wooded scenery—only open plains or treeless ridges bounding the horizon. The silent grandeur and solitude of a virgin forest inspires us almost with awe — much more so than even the broad expanse of the ocean. It conveys, also, involuntarily to our mind a feeling as if we were brought more closely before the Divine Power by whom the worlds without end were created, and before whom the proudest human work must sink into utter insignificance. No settlement, however princely — no city, however great its splendor, brilliant its arts, or enchanting its pleasures — can arouse those sentiments of veneration which, among all the grand works of nature, an undisturbed noble forest-region is most apt to call forth. I never saw truly happier homes of unmingled contentedness than in the seclusion of the woods. It is as if the bracing pureness of the air, the remoteness from the outer world, the unrestricted freedom from formal restraint, give to forest-life a charm for which in vain we will ever seek elsewhere. The forest inhabitant, as a rule, sees his life prolonged; an air of peace on all sides surrounds him; even with less prosperity, he is glad to

* *Sketch of the Life of Schiller*, by Sir Edward Bulwer Lytton, p. 2.

break away from the turmoils and enmities into which elsewhere he is thrown by the bustle and struggle of the world, and to seek again this calm retreat in forest mountains. The existence of many an invalid might be prolonged and rendered more enjoyable, while many a sufferer might be restored to health, were he to seek timely the patriarchal simplicity of forest life, and the pure air, wafted decarbonized in deli cious freshness through the forest, ever invigorating strength, restoring exhilaration and buoyancy of his mind. In this young country new lines of railway are early to disclose some of the almost paradisic fea tures of sylvan scenery, hitherto known to most of us only through the talent of illustrious landscape-paint ers of this city.

"To sit on rocks, to muse o'er flood and fell;
To slowly trace the forest's shady scene,
Where things that own not man's dominion dwell,
And mortal foot has ne'er or rarely been;
To climb the trackless mountain, all unseen,
With the wild flock, that never need a fold;
Alone o'er steep and foaming falls to lean—
This is not solitude: 'tis but to hold
Converse with nature's charms, and view her stores untold."

BYRON.

I regard the forest as an heritage given to us by Nature, not for spoil or to devastate, but to be wisely used, reverently honored, and carefully maintained. I regard the forests as a gift, intrusted to any of us only for transient care during a short space of time, to be surrendered to posterity again as an unimpaired property, with increased riches and augmented blessings to pass as a sacred patrimony from generation to generation.

ON THE

APPLICATION OF PHYTOLOGY

TO THE

INDUSTRIAL PURPOSES OF LIFE.

A POPULAR DISCOURSE,

Delivered at the Industrial Museum of Melbourne, on 3d November, 1870.

By Ferdinand von Mueller, C.M.G., M.D., Ph. D., F.R.S.

Comm. Ord., Santiago, Kn. of Orders of Austria, France, Prussia, Italy, Wuertemberg, Denmark, Mecklenburg, Gotha; Government Botanist for Victoria, and Director of the Botanic Gardens at Melbourne.

Called upon somewhat suddenly to choose the theme for the discourse of this evening, I made my choice unguardedly. I anticipated in my thoughts how, during the intended instructive recreation of this hour, the bearings of intimate botanic knowledge on many an industrial pursuit might readily be demonstrated by some impressive facts. But, on reflection, I saw myself at once surrounded by so varied and bewildering a multitude of objects that to do justice in a few words to my theme became a hopeless task. But while I offer this mere introductory address for a series of lectures on the phytologic section of this institution, we might learn by a rapid glance over an area of knowledge singularly wide that only through many successive discourses, explaining subjects in detail, the student can become aware of the importance of phytologic knowledge in its relation to the industrial purposes of life. In all zones, except the most icy, mankind depends on plants for its principal wants. For our sustenance, clothing dwellings, or utensils; for our means of transit, whether by sea or land; indeed, for all our ordinary daily requirements, we have to draw the material largely, and often solely, from the vegetable world. The resources for all these necessities must be—it cannot be otherwise—manifold in the extreme, and singularly varied, again, in different climatic zones, or under otherwise modified conditions.

To render, therefore, these vegetable treasures accessible to our fullest benefit, not only locally, but universally, must ever be an object of the deepest significance. Increasing requirements of the human races and augmented insight into the gifts of nature render now-a-days quite imperative the closest appliances of science to our resources and our daily wants.

"*Omnis tellus optima ferat!*" has become the motto of our Acclimatization Society; or let me quote from Virgil: "*Non omnis fert omnia tellus, hic segetes, illic veniunt felicius uvae.*" Striving to unite the products of many lands, it suffices for us nowhere any longer to discriminate among these resources with merely crude notions; but it becomes necessary to fix accurately, also, as far as plants are concerned, their industrial value, trace their origin, test their adaptability, investigate their productiveness, durability, qualities;

and to reduce all these inquiries to a sound basis by assigning to any species that position in the phytologic system by which it can be recognized by any one in any part of the globe. When the wants of phytoglaphy are satisfied we have to call to aid chemistry, therapy, geology, culture, microscoptic investigation, pictorial art, and other branches of knowledge, to illustrate the respective value of the species, and the degree of its importance to any particular community. But in the discussions of one evening we can do no more than to touch succinctly only on a few of those vegetable objects most promising to our own colony for introduction, or most accessible among those indigenous here; we may glance on them, also, with a view of learning how their elucidation might practically be pursued, and the knowledge thus gained be diffused. To aid in the latter aim the phytologic section in the Industrial Museum is to be established; of the requirements of this section I shall say a few passing words.

The products and educts of the vegetable world are immense; any display of them in the order of science, as intended for this museum, must carry with it a permanency of impressive instruction which any other modes of teaching, sure to be more ephemerous, fail to convey. But these efforts at diffusing knowledge should be seconded by means not inadequate to a great object, and should be worthy of the dignity and name of this rising country. Who would not like to see the best woods of every country stored up here in instructive samples—nearly a thousand kinds alone to choose from, as far as our continent is concerned? Who would not wish to have here at hand for comparison the barks, exudations, grains, drugs, as raw material? Who would not desire to have ready access to a series of oils, whether pressed or distilled, whether from indigenous or imported plants? Who would not have it in his power to compare the starches, dyes, casts of our luscious fruits, or the paper-material, tars, acids, coals of various kinds, fibers, alkaloids, and other medicinal preparations from various plants?

Why not place here a series of all the weapons and implements, traced accurately to their specific origin? From such even in many instances we have learned, through keen observations of the first nomadic occupants of the soil, the use of many kinds of wood. All these objects, crude or prepared in the multitudinous way of their adaptations, ought to be accompanied, wherever necessary, by full explanatory designations, microscopic sections, and other means of elucidation; while the periodic issue of descriptive indices, detailing still more copiously the derivation, uses, preparation, and monetary value of such objects, will enable us to serve the full intentions for which this museum section has been formed.

Lectures, however valuable, demonstrations, however instructive, cannot alone form the path of extensive industrial education; most minds, indeed, prefer to dwell tacitly on the objects of their choice, and muse quietly about the adaptability of any of them for operations or improvements in which they may be specially interested.

How many inventions have received their first impulse from an institution such as we wish to form! Investigators, eminent in their profession, will doubtless unite here, sooner or later, to bring to bear the sum of their knowledge, earned by a life-long toil, for giving vitality to that information which is to enter guidingly into the ordinary purposes of life. Thus, the happiness and prosperity of our fellow-men should be enhanced and exalted, and one of the loftiest objects of our striving after truths be fulfilled.

But the unassuming worker, conscious how far his own honest intentions advanced beyond his best results, may well exclaim with Moore, in his soft melodies :

> "Ah ! dreams too full of saddening truth,
> Those mansions o'er the main
> Are like the hopes I built in youth,
> As sunny, and as vain!"

Let us first take a glance at one of our innumerable forest glens. We see in the deep, rich detritus of rocks and fallen leaves, accumulated in past centuries some of the grandest features of the world's vegetation. Fern-trees* rise, at least exceptionally, to a height of eighty feet, higher, therefore, than any other parts of the globe, unless in Norfolk Island. Mammoth-Eucalypts abound, having, in elevation, rivals only in the Californian Sequoia Wellingtonia; we may, indeed, obtain, from one individual tree, planks enough to freight almost a ship of the tonnage of the *Great Britain.* Todea Ferns, now sought in trade, occur in these recesses, weighing, deprived of their fronds, almost a ton ; and, if the Xanthorrhœas do resemble, as popularly thought, our once spear-armed natives, then the Todea stems bear certainly as justly a resemblance to large black bears, as has been comically contended. The Fan Palms,† though

* Alsophila Australis, R. Br.

† Corypha (Livistona) Australis, R. Br.

only occurring in East Gipps Land, within our territory, rank among the most lofty of the globe, though also among the most hardy. All this, in our latitude, seem astounding — but more, it demonstrates, also, great riches; and I allude to it here only because I wished to show how a vegetation so prodigious points to the facilities of a natural, magnificent, industrial culture. The complex of vegetation is always an indicator of the soil and climate; as such alone, plants deserve close study. In this instance it reveals untold treasures, and yet, without phytographic knowledge they could never be understood, nor any intelligent appreciation of them be conveyed beyond the locality.

But can this grand picture of nature not be further embellished? Might not the true Tulip-tree, and the large Magnolias of the Mississippi and Himalaya, tower far over the Fern-trees of these valleys, and widely overshade our arborescent Labiatae?* Might not the Andine Wax Palm, the Wettinias, the Gingerbread Palm, the Jubea, the Nicau, the northern Sabals, the Date, the Chinese Fan Palms, and Rhapis flabelliformis, be associated with our Palm in a glorious picture? Or, turning to still more utilitarian objects, would not the Cork-tree, the Red Cedar, the Camphor-tree, the Walnuts and Hickories of North America, grow in these rich, humid dales, with very much greater celerity than even with all our tending in less genial spots? Could not, of four hundred coniferous trees, and three hundred sorts of Oaks, nearly every one be naturalized in these ranges, and thus

* Rhododendron arboreum attains a height of thirty feet, while Rh. Falconeri rises to fifty feet, with leaves half a yard long.

deals, select tanning material, cork, pitch, turpentine, and many other products be gained far more readily there than elsewhere in Victoria, from sources rendered our own? Ought we not to test in these valleys how far the Sisso, the Sal, the Teak, may prove hardy, and as important here as our Blackwood and Eucalypts abroad? Or shall I enumerate all the ornamental woods for furniture, machinery, instruments, which form an endless array of genera, and species might be chosen as introducable, indeed, from most lands ; many of these, perhaps, to find an asylum in our mountains before—like in St. Helena and other isolated spots—the remarkable and endemic trees are swept by man's destructive agency from the face of the globe ? Shall I speak in detail of the trees which yield dyes, and many medicinal substances ? If the Turkey Box-tree should continue the best for the wood-engraver, it would, in these valleys, assume its largest dimensions. I do not hesitate in affirming that out of ten thousand kinds of trees, which probably constitute the forests of the globe, at least three thousand would live and thrive in these mountains of ours ; many of them destined to live through centuries, perhaps, not a few through twice a thousand years, as great historic monuments. Within the railway-fences, hitherto in this respect unused, trees might be raised as materials for restoring, locally, the sleepers, posts, and rails, prior to their decay. The principles of physiology, the revelations of the microscope, aud the results of chemical tests guide us, not only in our selections of the trees, but often teach us, beforehand, the causes and reasons of durability or decay.

The longevity of certain kinds of trees is marvelous. British Oaks are estimated to attain an age of two thousand years. The Walnut-tree, the Sweet Chestnut, and Black Mulberry-tree, live through many centuries, if cared for. Wellingtonias are found to be one thousand one hundred years old. Even the South European Elm, which, since the time of the Romans, has also made Britain its home, is known to stand six hundred years. Dr. Hooker regards the oldest Cedars yet existing, at Mount Lebanon, as two thousand five hundred years old. Historic records are extant of Orange-trees having attained an age of seven hundred years, yet aged trees continue in full bearing, under favorable circumstances ; a single tree is said to have yielded, in a harvest, twenty thousand oranges. Individual Olive-trees are also supposed to have existed ever since the Christian era. The European Cypress, the British Yew, the Ginkgo, and the Kauri afford other remarkable instances of longevity.

The Date-Palm gratefully bears its rich crop of fruit for two hundred years. The Dragon-tree of Orotava is another familiar example of extraordinary longevity. Here, in Victoria, the native Beech, and several Eucalypts are veritable patriarchs of the forests, and of a far more venerable age than is generally supposed.

So much for the lasting of some of our work, to encourage planting operations.

If Cook, who stepped with the pride of an explorer on these shores precisely a century ago, could view once more the scene of his discoveries, he would be charmed by the sight of noble cities, and the happy aspect of rural industry; but he would turn his eyes in dismay from the desolation and aridity which a merciless sacrifice of the native forests has already so sadly brought about—a sacrifice arising from an utter absence of all thoughts for the future. Ever since antiquity this work of forest destruction has gone on in every country, until, sooner or later, such reckless improvidence has been overtaken by a resentful Nemesis, in hindering the progress of national prosperity, and the comfort of whole communities.

After lengthened periods of toil there partially arose, but partially only, what an early guardianship might have readily retained for most countries. When I largely shared in the labors of establishing, for Australian trees, a reputation abroad, I certainly did, also, entertain a hope to awaken here, likewise, a universal interest in the dissemination of an almost endless number of trees from the colder and subtropic girdles of the whole globe. (Vide Phil. Inst., 1858, pp. 93 to 109.) A few scattered trees are of no national moment. We want the massive upgrowth of the Pitch-pines, just as on the Pine barrens of the United States; we want whole forests of the Deal Pines, both cis and transatlantic; we want over all our mountains the Silver Fir, already the charm of the ancients; we want the Australian Red Cedar, scarcely any longer existing in its native haunts; we want the Yarrah-tree, forest-like, as in West Australia; we want the various elastic Ash-trees, which are so easily raised; we want, indeed, no end of other trees, because the greater part of Victoria is ill-wooded; because our climate is hot and dry; because extensive coal layers we have not yet found. What practical bearing can all the teaching in this hall, all the display in this museum, really exercise, if, finally, the artisan finds himself without an adequate and inexpensive material for his work? Annually, the timber of one hundred and fifty thousand acres is cut away in the United States to supply the want for railway-sleepers alone. The annual expenditure there in wood, for railway buildings and cars, is £7,600,000. In a single year the locomotives of the United States consume £11,200,000 of wood. The whole wood industries of the United States represent, now, an annual expenditure of one hundred million sterling. There, forty thousand artisans are engaged alone in woodwork. Here, in Victoria, notwithstanding the activity of many saw-mills, we imported, only last year, timber to the value of £270,572 for our own use. As these remarks may find publicity, I have appended further notes on timber-trees, eminently desirable for massive introduction, but do not wish to exhaust by details the patience of this audience.

But it would be vain to expect that Europe and America will continue forever to furnish for us their timber. The constantly-increasing population and the augmented requirements of advancing industries will render no longer yonder woods accessible also to us before the century passes, because even in those northern countries the timber supply will then barely satisfy local wants.

An idea may be formed of forest value when we enter on some calculations of the supply of timber or other products available from one of our largest Eucalyptus-trees. Suppose one of the colossal Eucalyptus amygdalina at the Black Spur was felled, and its total height ascertained to be four hundred and eighty feet, its circumference toward the base of the stem eighty-one feet, its lower diameter to be twenty-six feet, and at the height of three hundred feet its diameter six feet. Suppose *only half* the available wood was cut into planks of twelve inches width, we would get, in the terms of the timber trade, four hundred and twenty-six thousand seven hundred and twenty superficial feet at one inch thickness, sufficient to cover nine and three fourths acres. The same bulk of wood cut into railway-sleepers, six feet by six inches by eight inches, would yield in number seventeen thousand seven hundred and eighty. Not less than a length of twenty-three miles of three-rail fencing, including the necessary posts, could be constructed. It would require a ship of about one thousand tonnage to convey the timber and additional firewood of half the tree; and six hundred and sixty-six drayloads at one and one half tons would thus be formed to remove half the wood. The essential oil obtainable from the foliage of the whole tree may be estimated at thirty-one pounds; the charcoal, suppose there was no loss of wood, seventeen thousand nine hundred and fifty bushels; the crude vinegar, two hundred and twenty-seven thousand two hundred and sixty-nine gallons; the wood-tar, thirty-one thousand one hundred and fifty gallons; the potash, two tons eleven hundred weight. But how many centuries elapsed before undisturbed nature could build up by the subtle processes of vitality these huge and wondrous structures!

Some feelings of veneration and reverence should also be evinced toward the native vegetation, where it displays its rarest and grandest forms. It is lamentable that in all Australia scarcely a single spot has been secured* for preserving some relics of its most ancient trees to convey to posterity an idea of the original features of our primeval forests. Though it may appear foreign to my subject, I cannot withhold also on this occasion an imploring word, more particularly when I notice land-proprietors in East Australia to hold not even sacred a single native Banyan-tree, which required centuries for building its expansive dome and its hundreds of columnar pillars; nor to allow a single Cyrtosia Orchid to continue with its stem trailing to the length of thirty feet, and to remain with its thousands of large, fragrant blossoms, the pride of the forest. That very Cyrtosia gives a clue to the affinity and structure of other plants not nearer to us than Java; and its destruction, with probably that of many others which the naturalist forever is now prevented to dissect, or the artist to delineate, or the museum custodian to preserve, will be a loss to systematic natural history, also, forever. Again, in a spirit of Vandalism, a Fan-Palm, after a hundred years' growth, is no longer allowed to raise its slender stem and lofty crown in our own forests of Gipps Land, simply because curiosity is prompted to obtain a dishful of Palm-Cabbage at the sacrifice of a century's growth.

Let it be remembered that the uncivilized inhabitants of many a tropical country know how to respect the original and not always restorable gifts of a bountiful Providence. They will invaribly climb the Palm-

* On the River Hastings some magnificent dales have been lately protected by the Government of New South Wales for the sake of the incomparably beautiful and grand native vegetation, an example deserving extensive imitation. The forests of the Bunya Araucaria, occupying only a limited natural area, are also secured against intrusion by the Government.

tree to obtain its nuts or to plait its leaves; so, also a resident in our forests might obtain from a grove of our hardy Palms, if still any are left in this land of Canaan, an annual income by harvesting the seeds as one of the most costly articles of horticultural export.

Speaking of Palms, let me observe that the tall Wax Palm of New Granada (Ceroxlyon andicola) extends almost to the snow-line. It is needless to add that we might grow this magnificent product of andine vegetation in many localities of the country of our own adoption. Each stem yields annually about twenty-five pounds of a waxy, resinous coating, which when melted together with tallow forms an exquisite composition for candles. Chamærops Fortunei, a Chinese Fan Palm of considerable height, is here hardy, like in South Europe; so would be, probably, the Gingerbread Palm (Hyphaene Thebaica). Of the value of some Palms we may form an appreciation when we reflect that Elais Guineensis, which at the end of this century should be productive in Queensland and North-west Australia, yields from the fleshy outer portion of its nut the commercially famed Palm-oil, prepared much in the manner of Olive-oil; the value of this African Palm-oil imported in 1861 into England was two millions sterling, the demand for it for soap manufacture, and railway engines and carriages, being enormous.* The Chilean Jubaea or Coquito Palm grows spontaneously as far south as the latitude of Swan Hill, and is rich in a melliginous sap.† A Date Palm planted now would still be in full bearing two hundred years hence.

*The import of Palm-oil into Britain during 1868 was nearly a million cwt. (960.059 cwt.).

† Each tree yields ninety gallons of sap at a time, used for the preparation of palm-honey.

When hopeful illusion steps beyond the stern realities of the day, it cannot suppress a desire that enlightened statesmanship will always wisely foresee the absolute requirements of future generations. The colonist who lives in enjoyment of his property near the ranges and sees a flourishing family growing up around him, asks ominously what will be the aspect of these forests at the end of the century, if the present work of demolition continues to go on? He feels that though the forests not solely bring us the rain, through forests only a comparatively arid country can have the full advantage of its showers, as bitter experience has taught generation after generation since Julius Cæsar's time. The colonist reflects with apprehension that while no year nor day, when passed into eternity, can be regained, no provision whatever is made for the coming population, in whose welfare, perhaps as the head of a family, and perhaps even bearing political responsibility, he is interested. He would gladly co-operate in the labors of a local Forest Board, just like members of Road Boards and Shire Councils enter cheerfully on the special duties alloted to their administration. His local experience would dictate the rules under which in each district the timber and other products of the forest could be most lucratively utilized without desolation for the future; and he would be best able to judge, and to seek advice how the yield of the forest could be advantageously maintained, and its riches methodically be increased. All this will weigh more heavily on his mind when he is cognizant that even in Middle Europe, in countries so well provided with coals, and of a much cooler clime than ours, the extent of the forests is kept scrupulously intact, and their regular yield remains secured from year to year and from century to century. He would rest satisfied if only the trifling revenue of the forests could be applied by him and his neighbors to an inexpensive restoration of the woods consumed. He would delight in seeing the leading foreign timber trees disseminated with our own Red Gum-tree, Red Cedars, Yarrahs or Blackwoods, not by hundreds but in time to come by millions, well aware that the next generations may either censure reproachfully the shortcomings of their ancestors, or may point gratefully to the results of an earnest and well-sustained foresight of future wants. As a first step, at least in each district a few square miles should be secured for subsequent forest nurseries in the best localities, commanding irrigation by gravitation, and ready access also, before it is too late, and all such spots are permanently alienated from the Crown.

Physical science must yet largely be called to our experimental aid before we can dispel the many crude notions in reference to the effect of forest vegetation on climate in all its details. It is thus a startling fact, as far as experiments under my guidance hitherto could elucidate the subject, that on a sunny day the leaves of our common Eucalypts and Casuarinas exhale a quantity of water several times, or even many times, larger than those of the ordinary or South European Elm, English Oak, or Black Poplar; while from the foliage of our native Silver Wattle only half, or even less than half, the quantity of water is evaporated than from the Poplar or Oak. This degree of exhalation, so different in various trees, depends on the number, position, and size of their stomata, and stands in immediate correlation to the power of absorption of moisture. Besides, if the evaporation of Eucalyptus-trees is so enormous during heat, and if the often horizontal roots of these trees thus render soil around them very dry, in consequence of the copious conveyance of moisture to the air, they simultaneously, by the rapidity of their evaporation in converting aqueous to gaseous liquid, or water into vapor, cause a lowering of the temperature most important in our climate during the months of extreme heat, while their capability of absorbing moisture during rain or from humid air must be commensurately great.

It is beyond the scope of this address to dwell further on facts like these; but I was anxious to demonstrate by a mere example how much we have yet to learn by patient research before we will have recognized in all its details the important part which forest vegetation plays in the great economy of nature. Concerning forest culture, I would very briefly allude to an instance showing how, by the teachings of natural science and thoughtful circumspection, the rewards of industrial pursuits may become surprisingly augmented. In the uplands of the Madras Presidency, an ingenious method has been adopted in gathering the harvest of Cinchona-bark, in recent very extensive plantations, by removing it in strips without destroying the cambium layer. Then, by applying moss to the denuded part of the stem, not only is the removed portion of the bark renewed within a year, to the thickness of three years' growth, but the protection of the tender bark against the influence of light and air allows nearly all the quinine and other alkaloids to remain retained in the cortical layer without decomposition, while in the ordinary three years' bark half or more of these principles is lost.

Facts like these lead us to appreciate the important bearings of the natural sciences on all branches of industry; but they warn us, also, to pause before we give our further consent to the unlimited and reckless demolition of our most accessible forest lands, on the maintenance of which so many of our industries depend.

Just as it required, even under undisturbed favorable influences, centuries before our forest riches were developed to their pristine grandeur, so it will need, in the ordinary laws of nature, at least an equal lengthened period before we can see towering up again the sylvan colosses, which eminently contributed to the fame of the natural history of this land—if, indeed, the altered physical condition of the country will render the restoration of the trees on a grand scale possible at all.

Has science drawn in vain its isothermal girdles around the globe, or has the searching eye of the philosopher in vain penetrated geologic structure, or in vain the exploring phytographer circumscribed the forms? Well do we know what and where to choose; botanic science steps in to define the objects of our choice, which other branches of learning teach us to locate and rear.

The Tea would as thriftly luxuriate in our wooded valleys as in its native haunts at Assam, and yield a harvest far more prolific than away from the ranges. Indeed, we may well foresee that many forest slopes will be dotted in endless rows with the bushes of the

Tea, precisely as our drier ridges are verdant with the vine. Erythroxylon-Coco, the wondrous stimulating plant of Peru, should be raised in the mildest and most sheltered forest glens, where the stillness of the air excludes the possibility of cutting frosts. Hop, cultivated as a leading industry in Tasmania since a quarter of a century, will also take a prominent place on the brooks of our mountains. Peru-bark trees of various kinds should in spots so favored be subjected to culture trials. How easily could any swampy depression, not otherwise readily of value, be rendered productive by allowing plants of the handsome New Zealand flax lily quietly to spread as a source for future wealth. How far the demand of material for industrial purposes may quickly exceed the supply may be strikingly exemplified by the fact that hundreds of vessels are exclusively employed for bringing the Esparto grass (not superior to several of our most frequent sedges) from Spain to England, to augment the supply of rags for the endless increasing requirements of the paper-mills. Conversion of manifold material, even saw-dust, into paper, is carried on to a vast extent; a multitude of samples placed here before you will help to explain how wide the scope for paper material may extend. But the factories want material, not only cheap, but readily convertible, and adapted to particular working.

In all these selections, a few glances through the microscope, and the result of a few chemical reactions taught in this hall, may at once advise the artisan in his choice.

Phytologic inquiry is further to teach us rationally the nature of maladies to which plants are subject, just as it discloses even the sources of many of the most terrific and ravaging diseases of which the human frame is the victim. The microscope, that marvelous tool for discovery, has become, also, the guardian of many an industry. The processes of morbid growth, or the development and diffusion of the minute organism, between which descriptive botany knows how to discriminate, are thus traced out as the subtle and insidious causes which at times involve losses that count by hundreds of thousands in a single year, even in our yet small communities. But while the microscope discloses the form and development of the various minute organisms which cause, through the countless numbers of individuals, at times the temporary ruin of many branches of rural industry, it leaves us not helpless in our insight how to vanquish the invaders. In correctly estimating the limits of the specific forms, calling forth or concomitant with some of the saddest human maladies, phytography shares in the noble aim of alleviating human sufferings, or restoring health and prolonging vital existence.

But it comes most prominently within the scope of this Industrial Museum to delineate for the agricultural and forest section, in explanatory plates, the morbid processes under which crops and timber may succumb, and an industry be paralyzed or a country be verily brought to famine ; it devolves on us, also, simultaneously to explain the effect of remedial agents, such as sound reasoning from inductive science suggests or confirms. To array samples of all field products which our genial clime allows us to raise is doubtless the object of an instructive institution, more particularly in a young country, to which immigration streams mainly from a colder zone; but this display of increased capabilities, and of more varied products of a mostly winterless land, may entice the inexperienced to new operations without guarding him against failures. I should even like to see tables of calculations in this Museum, from which could be learned the yield and value of any crop within a defined acreage and from a soil chemically examined; but from this I would regard inseparable a close calculation of the costs under which each particular crop can only be raised. Unfortunately, surprising data are often furnished concerning the productiveness of new plants of culture; but it is as frequently forgotten that the large yield is, as a rule, dependent on an expenditure commensurately large.

Among the most powerful means for fostering phytologic knowledge for local instructive purposes, that of forming collections of the plants themselves remains one of the foremost. No school of any great pretension should be without a local collection of museum plants, nor should any mechanics' institute be without such. It serves as a means of reference most faithfully; it need not be a source of expenditure; it might be gathered as an object of recreation; it may add even to the world's knowledge. Through the transmission of numbered duplicate sets of plants to my office the accurate naming may be secured.* From such a normal collection in each district the inhabit-

* Parcels of plants pressed and dried, and afterward closely packed, can be inexpensively forwarded by post, and, by the excellence of the Australian postal arrangements, can be sent from distant stations of the interior, from whence botanical specimens of any kind, for ascertaining the nature and range of the species, are most acceptable; while full information on such material will at once be rendered.

ant may learn to discriminate at once with exactness between the different timber-trees, the grasses, the plants worthy of ornamental culture, or any others possessing industrial or cultural interest. The sawyer, as well as the trader in timber, may learn how many of the one hundred and forty Australian Eucalypts occur within his reach — how phytography designates each of them by a specific appellation acknowledged all over the globe. Phytologic inquiry, aided by collateral sciences, will disclose to him beforehand the rules for obtaining the wood at the best seasons, for selecting it for special purposes, for securing the best preservation. Phyto-chemistry will explain to him what average percentage of potash, oils, tar, vinegar, alcohol, tannic acid, etc., may be obtained under ordinary circumstances from each. He will understand, for instance, that the so-called Red Gum-tree of Victoria, the one so famed for the durability of its wood and for the peculiar medicinal astringency of its gum-resin, is widely different from the tree of that vernacular named in Western Australia; that it is wanting in Tasmania, yet that it has an extensive geographic range over the interior of our continent; and that thus the experiences gained on the products of this particular species of tree by himself or others are widely applicable elsewhere. Through collections of these kinds the thoughtful colonist may have his attention directed to vegetable objects of great value in his own locality, of the existence of which he might otherwise not readily become aware. New trades may spring up, new exports may be initiated, new local factories be established. Phytographic works on Australian plants, now extant in many volumes, can readily be attached and rendered explanatory of such collections. A prize held out by the patrons of any school might stimulate the juvenile gatherer of plants to increased exertions; his youthful mind will be trained to observation and reflection and the faculties of a loftier understanding will be raised.

To the adult also, and particularly often to the invalid, new sources of enjoyment may thus be disclosed. What formerly was passed by unregarded will have a meaning; every blade over which he stepped thoughtlessly before will have a new interest; and even what he might have admired will gain additional charm; but while penetrating wonders he never dreampt of before he ought piously to ask who called them forth?

"Bright flowers shall bloom wherever we roam,
A voice Divine shall talk in each stream;
The stars shall look like worlds of love,
And this earth shall be one beautiful dream."

Thos. Moore's Irish Melodies.

What one single plant may do for the human race is perhaps best exemplified by the Cotton-plant. The Southern States of North America sent to England in 1860 nearly half a million tons of cotton (453,522 tons), by which means, in Britain alone, employment was given to about a million of people engaged in industries of this fabric, producing cotton goods to the value of £121,364,458. From rice, which like cotton will mature its crop in some of the warmer parts of Victoria,* sustenance is obtained for a greater number of human beings than from any other plant. In

* Particularly if the hardy mountain rice of China and Japan is chosen, which required no irrigation. The ordinary rice has been grown as far north as Lombardy,

the greater part of the Australian continent, where-ever water supply could be commanded, the rice would luxuriate. I found it wild in Arnheim's Land in 1855. Of sugar-cane the hardier varieties may within Victoria succeed in East Gipps Land and other warmer spots. Great Britain imported in 1863 not less than five hundred and eighty-six thousand six hundred tons.* Even our young colony imported last year to the value of nearly a million sterling (£948,329). Think of the commerce in other vegetable products, such as require in different places our local fostering care in order to add still more to our resources. Of various tobaccos we imported into Victoria in 1869 (deducting exports) to the value of £83,788; of wine, £84,687; of cereals, £781,250; of paper, £123,158. I will not enter on any remarks about sugar-beet, on which one of our fellow-colonists has lately compiled an excellent treatise. Of tea, in 1865, Britain required for home consumption eighty-five millions of lbs.† What a prospect for tea growth in Victoria, where this bush cares neither for the scorching heat of the Summer nor for the night-frosts of our lower regions; whereas, in the forest glens of our country, Tasmania, and elsewhere, the Tea-bush would yield most prolific harvests. Test plantations for manifold new cultures were recommended by me years ago in one of my official reports to the Legisla-

*"The total import of sugar into Britain was, during 1868, six hundred and twenty-six thousand three hundred and one tons; during 1869, six hundred and five thousend one hundred and twenty-nine tons."

† The total import of tea into Britain was—

During 1865	121,156,712 lbs.
" 1866	139,610,044 "
" 1867	128,028,726 "
" 1868	154,845,863 "
" 1869	139,223,298 "

ture; one plantation for the desert, one for subalpine regions, one for the deep valleys of the woodlands. The two latter might be in close vicinity at the Black Spur, and thus within the reach of ready traffic. The outlay in each case would be modest indeed. What an endless number of new industrial plants might thus be brought together within a few hours' drive of the city, under all the advantages of rich soil, shelter, and irrigation! What an attractive collection for the intelligent and studious might thus be permanently formed.

I will not weary this audience by giving a long array of names of any plants resisting alpine Winters, such as in our snow-clad higher mountains they would have to endure. We know that the Apple will live where even the hardy Pear will succumb; both will still thrive on our alpine plateaus. The Larch, struggling in vain with the dry heat of our open lowlands, would be a tree of comparatively rapid growth near alpine heights. The Birch, in Greenland, the only tree in Italy ascending to six thousand feet, in Russia the most universal, and there yielding for famed tanning processes its valued bark, is living—to quote the forcible remarks of an elegant writer—"is living on the bleak mountain sides from which the sturdy Oak shrinks with dismay." Add to it, if you like, the Paper-Birch, and a host of arctic, andine, and other alpine trees and bushes. Disseminate the Strawberries of the countries of our childhood, naturalize the Blackberry of northern forest moors. The American Cranberry-bush (Vaccinium macrocarpum), with its large fruits, is said to have yielded on boggy meadows, such as occupy a large terrain of the Australian

Alps, fully one hundred bushels on one acre in a year, worth so many dollars. If once established, such a plant would gradually spread on its own account for the benefit of future highland inhabitants. The Sugar Maple would seek these cold heights, to be tapped when the Winter snow melts. For half a century it will yield its saccharine sap, equal to several pounds of sugar annually.

Let us translocate ourselves now for a moment to our desert tracts, changed as they will likely be many years hence, when the waters of the Murray River, in their unceasing flow from snowy sources, will be thrown over the back plains, and no longer run entirely into the ocean, unutilized for husbandry. The lagoons may then be lined, and the fertile depressions be studded with the Date Palm ; Fig-trees, like in Egypt planted by the hundreds of thousands to increase and retain the rain, will then also have ameliorated here the clime ; or the White Mulberry-tree will be extensively extant then instead of the Mallee scrub ; not to speak of the Vine, in endless variety, nor to allude to a copious culture of Cotton in those regions. To Fig-trees and Mulberry-trees I refer more particularly, because it must be always in the first instance the object to raise in masses those utilitarian plants which can be multiplied with the utmost ease, and without any special skill, locally, and which, moreover, as in this case, would resist the dry heat of our desert clime. When recommending such a culture for industrial pursuits, it is not the aim to plant by the thousand, but by the million. Remember, also, that a variety of the Morus Alba occurs in Affghanistan, with a delicious fruit ; and that the importation of Figs into Britain alone, from countries in climate alike to large tracts of Victoria, has been of late years about one thousand tons annually. What the Fig-tree has effected for rainless tracts of Egypt is now on historic record.

I have spoken of horticultural industries as not altogether foreign to this institution—indeed, as representing a rising branch of commerce. Were I to enter on details of this subject the pages of this address might swell to a volume. But this I would mention, that in our young country the manifold facilities for rearing exotic plants in specially selected and adapted localities could only as yet receive imperfect consideration. We have, however, ample opportunities of selecting genial spots for the growth of such singular curiosities as the Flytrap plant (Dionæa Muscipula), and the Pitcher-plants (Sarracenias) of the bogs and swamps of the pine barrens and savannahs of Carolina, if we proceed to moory portions of our springy forest land. There is no telling, too, whether the Pitcher-plants of Khasya and China (species of Nepenthes) could not readily be grown and multiplied in similar localities, and the hardier of grand Epiphytes among the orchids, such as the subalpine Oncidium Warczewickyi, of Central America, which might readily be reared in our glens by horticultural enterprise, together with all the hardier Palms which modern taste has so well adopted for the ready decoration of dwelling-rooms.

Such plants as the Beaucarnea recurvata of Mexico, with its five thousand flowers in a single panicle, and the hardier Vellozias, from the bare mountain regions of Brazil, would endure our open air; while the innumerable South African Heaths, Stapeliæ, the Mesembryanthema, Pelargonia, lily-like plants, and many others, once the pride of European conservatories, can, with increased sea traffic, now gradually be introduced as beautifnl objects of trade into this country, where they need no glass protection. It leads too far to speak of the still more readily accessible numerous showy plants of South-west Australia, but among which, as a mere instance, the gorgeous Anigozanthi, the lovely Stylidia, the gay Banksiæ, and the fragrant Boronias may be mentioned.

Before leaving this topic, I may remind you that many esculent plants of foreign countries are deserving yet of test culture, and, perhaps, general adoption in this country. The Dolichos sesquipedalis, of South American, is a bean, cultivated in France on account of its tender pod. The Arracha esculenta, an umbellate from the cooler mountains of Central America, yields there, for universal use, its edible root. The climbing Chocho, of West India (Sechium edule), proved hardy in Madeira, and furnishes a root and fruit both palatable and wholesome. Vigna subterranea is the Earth Nut of Natal. The Taro of Tahiti (Calocasi macrorrhiza), though perfectly enduring our lowland clime, is, as yet, with allied species, but little cultivated — neither the Soja of Japan (Glycine Soja), nor the Caper of the Mediterranean. The Seakales (Crambe Maritima and C. Tatarica) might be naturalized on our sandy shores.

Regarding fibres, much yet requires to be effected by capitalists and cultivators, to turn such plants as the Grasscloth shrub, which I distributed for upward of a dozen years, to commercial importance for factories. A kind of Jute (Corchorus olitorius) succeeds as far north as the Mediterranean, and grows wild with the Sun Hemp (Crotalaria juncea) in tropical Australia; the latter plant comes naturally almost to the boundaries of our colony. A Melbourne rope-factory offers £36 for the ton of New Zealand Flax, and can consume six tons per week. Hemp, used since antiquity, produces, along with its fibre, the Hypnotic Churras. England imported, in 1858, Hemp, to the value of more than £1,000,000.* This may suffice to indicate new resources in this direction. For Sumach our country offers, in many places, the precise conditions for its successful growth, as confirmed by actual tests. Tannic substances, of which the indigenous supply is abundant and manifold, would assume still greater commercial importance by simple processes of reducing them to a concentrated form. How on any forest river might not the Filbert-tree be naturalized; on precipitous places, among rocks, it would form a useful jungle, furnishing, besides, its nuts, the material for fishing-rods, hoops, charcoal crayons, and other purposes. From a single forest at Barcelona sixty thousand bushels are obtained in a year. (For these and many other data brought before you in this lecture you may refer further, most conveniently, to a posthumous work of the great Professor Lindley, *Treasury of Botany*, edited by Mr. Th. Moore, with the aid of able contributors.) Even the Loquat would attain in our forest glens the size of a fair, or even large tree.

* The import of Hemp and Jute into Britain during 1868 was three million two hundred and eighty-one thousand two hundred and sixty-eight hundred weight; during 1869, three million five hundred and fifty-one thousand eight hundred and thirty-eight hundred weight. The undressed Hemp imported in 1868 was valued at £2,022,419.

Osiers and other willows used for basket-work, for charcoal, or for the preparation of salicine, might line any river banks, quite as much for the sake of shade and consolidation of the soil as for their direct utilitarian properties. In the forest ranges any dense line of Willows and Poplars will help to check the spread of the dreadful conflagrations in which so much of the best timber is lost, and through which the temperature of the country is for days heightened to an intolerable degree far beyond the scenes of devastation, while injuries are inflicted far and wide to the labors in the garden or the field. In the most arid deserts the medicinal Aloes might readily be established, to yield by a simple process the drug of commerce. Gourds of half a hundred weight have been obtained in Victoria, and show what the plants of the Melon tribe might do here, like in South Africa, for eligible spots in the desert land. Among the trees for those arid tracts, the glorious Grevillea robusta, with its innumerable trusses of fiery red, and its splendid wood for staves, is only one of the very many desirable; just as in the oases the Carob-tree will live without water, uninjured, because its deeply-penetrating roots render it fit to resist any drought. But it may be said that much that I instance is well known and well recorded—so, doubtless, it is, in the abstract—but variety requires to be distinguished from variety, species from species, and their geography, internal structure and components need carefully to be set forth, before any industry relating to plants can be raised on sound ground in proper localities, and be brought to its best fruitfulness.

Even a pond, a streamlet—how, with intelligent

foresight, may it be utilized and rendered lucrative to industry! The Water Nuts,* naturally distributed through large tracts of Europe and Asia, afford at Cashmere alone, for five months in the year, a nutritious and palatable article of food for thirty thousand people. Can the Menyanthes not be made a native here—one of the loveliest of water-plants, one of the best of tonics? The true Bamboo, which I first proved hardy here, used for no end of purposes by the ingenious Chinese—can we not plant it here at each dwelling, at each stream, a grateful yielder to industrial wants, not requiring itself any care—an object destined to embellish whole landscapes? An Arundinaria Bamboo from Nepal (A. falcata) proved very tall and quite hardy, even in Britain; and yet taller is the Mississippi Arundinaria (A. macrosperma)—indeed, rivaling in height the gigantic Chinese or Indian Bamboo.

Imagine how there might arise on the bold rocky declivities of the Grampians the colossal columns of the Cereus giganteus of the extra-tropic Colorado regions—huge candelabras of vegetable structure, which would pierce the roof of our museum hall if planted on the floor, and would be as expansive in width as the pedestal of the monument consecrated to our unfortunate explorers. Picture to yourselves an Echinocactus Visnago of New Mexico, lodged in the wide chasm of our Pyrenees, one of these monsters weighing a ton, and expanding into a length of nine feet, with a diameter of three feet. Think of such plants mingled with the Canarian Dragon-tree, one of which is supposed to have lived from our

* Several species of Trapa.

Redeemer's time to this age, because four centuries effected on these Giant Lilies but little change. Welwitchia here, like in rainless Damaraland, might grow in our desert sands as one of the most wonderful of plants, its only pair of leaves being cotyledonous and lasting well-nigh through a century. Or associate in your ideas with these one of the medicinal Tree Aloes of Namaqua, or one of the Poison Euphorbias, never requiring pluvial showers (Euphorbia grandidens), some as high as a good-sized two-storied dwelling-house; transfer to them also Cereus senilis, thirty feet high, which, with all its attempts to look venerable, only suceeds to be grotesque; add to these extraordinary forms such Lily-trees as the Fourcroya longæva, with a stem of forty feet and an inflorescence of thirty feet, whereas Agave Americana, Agave Mexicana and allied species, while they quietly pass through the comparatively short space of time allotted to their existence, weave in the beautiful internal economy of their huge leaves the threads which are to yield the tenacious Pita-cords, so much in quest for the rope-bridges of Central America.

Some of the Echinocacti extend as far south as Buenos Ayres and Mendoza, and would introduce into many arid tracts of Victoria, together with the almost numberless succulents of South Africa, a great ornamental attraction, which horticultural enterprise might turn to lucrative account; just like our native showy plants will become objects of far higher commercial importance than hitherto has been attached to them. The columns of Cereus Peruvianus rise sometimes to half a hundred feet; some Cacteæ are in reality the vegetable fountains of the desert. Such plants as Echinocactus platyceras, with its fifty thousand thorns and setæ, should be cultivated in our open grounds for horticultural trade, whereas the Cochineal Cacti (Opuntia Tuna, O. coccinellifera and a few other species), might well be still further distributed here, in order that food may be available for the cochineal insects when other circumstances in Australia will become favorable for the local production of this costly dye.

These are a few of many instances which might be adduced to demonstrate how the landscape pictures of Victoria might be embellished in another century, and new means of gain be obtained from additional manifold resources.

But while your thoughts are carried to other zones and distant lands, let us not lose sight of the reason for which we assembled, namely, to deal with utilitarian objects and the application of science thereon. All organic structures, however, whether giants or pigmies, whether showy or inconspicuous, have their allotted functions to fulfill in nature, are destined to contribute to our wants, are endowed with their special properties, are heralding the greatness of the Creator. But here in this hall I would like to see displayed by pictorial art the most majestic forms in nature, were it only to delineate for the studious the physiognomy of foreign lands, irrespective of any known industrial value of the objects thus sketched. The painter's art in choosing from nature does impress us most lastingly with the value and grandeur of its treasures. Each plant, as it were, has a history of discovery of its own; who would not like to trace it? And this again brings us face to face with those who carried before us the torch of scientific inquiry into the dark recesses of mystery, and shed a flood of light on perhaps long-concealed magnificence and beauty. The youth, aroused to the sublime feeling of wishing at least to follow great men in independent researches, may be animated if in a hall like this each division were ornamented with the portraits of the foremost of those discoverers who through ages advanced knowedge to the standard of the present day.

> "Deeds of great men all remind us
> We can make our lives sublime,
> And departing leave behind us
> Footprints on the sands of time.
>
> "Though oft depressed and lonely,
> Our fears are laid aside,
> If we remember only
> Such also lived and died.
>
> "Learn from the grand old masters,
> Or from the bard sublime,
> Whose distant footsteps echo
> Through the corridor of time."

LONGFELLOW.

Discovery proceeds step by step. Commenced by original thinkers, enlarged by sedulous experimenters, fostered by the thoughtful portion of the community, and by any administration of high views, it is utilized by well-directed enterprise, and marches onward steadily in its progress. Guttenberg and his collaborators gave us the printing art, which has done more to enlighten the world than all other mechanisms taken together; and though four centuries have altered much in the speed and cost of producing prints, they have not materially changed the forms of this glorious art, as the beautifully-decorated pages of the earliest printed Bibles testify. Thus we have reason to be yet daily grateful for this invaluable gain from the genius of days long passed.

Thoughtless criticism is but too often impatient of success, and demands results premature and unreasonable. Incompetent and perversive censure may even carry the sway of public opinion—misleading, and misled; and, still worse, organized tactics may apply themselves, for sinister purposes of their own, to disturb the quiet work of the discoverer, mar the results of his labors, or paralyze the vitality of research, not understanding, or not wishing to understand, its direction or its object.

And yet, should we have no faith in science, whether it reveals to us the minutest organisms in a perfection unalterable, * or the grandest doctrines of truth, sure ever to bear on human happiness and the peace of our soul; should we have no faith in science, whether it unravels the metallic treasures of the depth and the coals of the forests of bygone ages, or by eternal laws permits us to trace the orbits of endless celestial worlds through space; no faith, if it allows us through spectroscopic marvels to count unerringly the billions of oscillations of each ray of dispersed light within a second; or if it discloses the chemism of distant worlds, and therewith an applicability of research, both tellural and sidereal, ever endless and inexhaustible. Science, as the exponent of God-like

* As an instance of the marvelous complexity, and yet exquisite perfection of the minutest creatures, the organ of vision in insects may be adduced. Most careful observers have ascertained that the eyes of very many insects are compound, contain numerous eyelets; each of these provided with a distinct cornea, lens, iris, pupil, and a whole nervous apparatus. In our despised ordinary house-fly may be counted about four thousand of these most subtle instruments of vision; in some dragon-flies about twelve thousand. Reliable microscopists have counted even seventeen thousand three hundred and fifty-five in a kind of butterfly, while in the beetle genus mordella these most delicate eyelets have been found to rise to the almost incredible number of twenty - five thousand and eighty - eight.—(*From Th. Rym, Jones.*)

laws, draws us in deepest veneration to the power divine. That is true science!

"As into tints of sevenfold ray
 Breaks soft the silvery shimmering white;
As fade the sevenfold tints away,
 And all the rainbow melts in light;
So from the Iris sportive call
 Each magic tint the eye to chain,
And now let truth unite them all,
 And light its single stream regain."

—*Bulwer Lytton, from Schiller.*

If a series of experiments with coloring principles from coal-tar and bituminous substances led to the invention of the brilliant aniline colors, and brought about an almost total change in many dye processes, how many new wonders may not be disclosed to technology by the rapid strides of organic chemistry? As is well-known, three or four chemic elements are only engaged in forming numberless organic compounds, by a slight increase or decrease or rearrangement of the atomic molecules, constructing, for instance, from these three or four elements, ever present and ever attainable, the deadly hydrocyanic acid, the terrible atropin, or the dreadful aconitin at one time; or at another time, harmless ammonia combinations universally used for culinary and other purposes of daily life. Our wood-tars, we may remember, are left, as yet, almost unexamined as regards their chemic constitutents. Few of our timbers have been chemically analyzed; few other of our vegetable products are as yet accurately tested. What an endless expanse for exploration does organic chemistry thus offer us! We are called on, among a thousand things, to trace out similar mutual relation and counteraction of such extremely powerful plants as the

Belladonna and Calabar Bean. Here medicine, chemistry, and phytology go hand in hand. How, again, is any analysis of the chemic constituents of any plant, for cultural purposes or otherwise, to be applied, unless we command a language of phytographic expressions which will name with never-failing precision the object before us, and give to its elucidation value and stability ?

We may speak chemically of potash plants, lime plants, and so forth ; we may wish to define thereby the direction of certain industrial pursuits, and we may safely thereby foretell what plants can be raised profitably on any particular soil or with the use of any particular manure ; but how is this knowledge to be fixed without exact phytologic information, or how is the knowledge to be applied, if we are to trust to vernacular names, perplexing even within the area of a small colony, and useless, as a rule, beyond it ? Colonial Box-trees by dozens, yet all distinct, and utterly unlike Turkey Box ; colonial Myrtle, without the remotest resemblance to the poet's myrtle ; colonial Oaks, analogous to those Indian trees which as Casuarinæ were distinguished so graphically by Rumpf two hundred years ago, but without a trace of similarity to any real Oak—afford instances of our confused and ludicrous vernacular appellations. A total change is demanded, resting on the rational observations and deductions which science already has gained for us. Assuredly, with any claims to ordinary intelligence, we ought to banish such designations, not only from museum collections, but also from the dictionary of the artisan.

One of the genera of Mushrooms, certainly the

largest of them (Agaricus), contains alone about a thousand species, well distinguished from each other, a good many even occurring in this country. For the practical purposes of common life it becomes an object to distinguish the many wholesome from the multitude of deleterious kinds, or the circumstances under which the harmless sorts may become hurtful. In France the cultivation of mushrooms in under-ground caverns has become a branch of industry not altogether unimportaut. How, in other instances, is many a culinary vegetable to be distinguished from the poison herb without the microscope of the phytographer being applied to dissections, or without the language of science recording the characters ? How many a life, lost through a child's playfulness, or through the unacquaintance of the adult, even with the most ordinary objects of knowledge among plants, might have been saved, even in these times of higher education, if phytologic knowledge was more universal ! The species of fungi which can be converted into pleasant, nutritious food are far more numerous than popularly supposed, but for extending industries in this direction botanic science must assume the guardianship. In a technologic hall like this I should like to see instructive portraits also of all the edible and noxious plants likely to come within the colonist's reach.

Among about one thousand kinds of Fig-trees which (so Mons. Alphonse de Candolle tells me), through Mons. Bureau's present writings for the Prodromus, are ascertained to exist, only one yields the fig of our table, only one forms the famed sycamore fig, planted along so many roads of the Orient; only one constitutes our own *Ficus macrophylla*, destined, in its unsurpassed magnificence, to overshade here our pathways. How are these thousands of species of Ficus, all distinct in appearance, in character, and in uses—how are they to be recognized, unless a diagnosis of each becomes carefully elaborated and recorded, headed by a specific name ?

Without descriptive botany all safe discrimination becomes futile. To bear our share in building up an universal system of specific delimitation of all plants is a task well worthy of the patronage of an intelligent and high-minded people. The physician is thereby guided to draw safe comparisons in reference to the action of herbs and roots which he wishes to prescribe, as available from native resources. Thus it was through Victorian researches that not only the close affinity of Goodeniaceæ to the order of Gentianeæ was brought to light, but simultaneously a host of herbs and shrubs of the former order gained for therapeutic uses. When once it was ascertained that the so-called Myrtle-tree of our forest moors was a true Beech the artisan then also found offered to him a timber of great similarity to that of the Beech forests of his British home.

Of the grass genus Panicum we know the world possesses, according to a recent botanic disquisition, about eight hundred and fifty species, all more or less nutritive. But one only of these is the famous Coapin of Angola (Panicum spectabile), one of the Warree (Panicum miliaceum), one the Bhadlee (Panicum pilosum), one the Derran (P. frumentaceum). We might dispense, perhaps, as far as these few are concerned, with their scientific appellations, though not even the mere task of naming has become therewith easier, and no information whatsoever of their characteristics has been gained. But if we wish to refer to any of the many hundred other species of Panicum, in what way are we to express ourselves if even their vernacular names could be collected from at least a dozen of languages, and impressed on any one's memory? They are, as may readily be imagined, very different indeed in their special nutritiveness, degree of endurance, and length of life. Of one hundred and forty species of Bromus only one is the Prairie Grass, which has attained already a great celebrity as a pasture grass naturalized in this country; and it is only one other Bromus, among the many nutritious kinds, which carries the palm as the most fattening fodder-grass for cold, marshy pastures, and gradually, through depasturing, suppresses completely all other grasses and weeds; so it is proved on the marshlands of Oldenburg. This Bromus (B. secalinus), as far as I am cognizant, is nowhere as yet economically cultivated in Victoria.

Nothing would be easier than to commence disseminating a number of the best grasses in addition to those already here; for instance, the Canadian Rice-Grass (Hydropyrum esculentum) for our swamp-lands. Their nutritive value must be tested by analysis and other experiments, just like that of the Saltbushes of the Murray Flats. Hence ample scope for the exertions of science also in this direction.

In Cotta's celebrated publishing establishment at Stuttgart a most useful work is issued by my friend, Prof. Noerdlinger, on the structure of timber of various kinds, illustrated by microscopic sections of the wood itself; for the latter fascicles I furnished some material from this colony. The work should be accessible in this Museum to all interested in woodwork.

How much we have yet to learn of the value of our forest products is instanced when we now know from Spanish physicians to combat ague with Eucalyptus-leaves, or when Count Maillard de Marafy, from experiments instituted this year in Egypt, announced to us that Eucalyptus-leaves can be used as a substitute for Sumach. (Egypte Agricole, 1870.)

Already, in the earlier part of this lecture, I spoke of the Peru Bark plants; but the Cinchonas are not all of the same kind. Some endure a lower degree of temperature than others, some are richer in quinine, others richer in cinchonine, others in quinoidine; and this again is much subject to fluctuations under different effects of climate and soil. Great errors may be committed, and have been committed, by adopting from among a number of species the least valuable, or one under ordinary circumstances almost devoid of alkaloid, though a representative of the genus cinchona, and not unlike the lucrative species. When calculations in India prognosticate the almost incredible annual return of one hundred and thirty per cent., after four years, on the original outlay for Cinchona plantation, it is supposed that the conditions for this new industrial culture are to the utmost favorable. That one of the best species did not thrive there at all in proportion to expectations is owing, in my opinion, to geologic conditions. The Cinchonas before you, reared in soil from our Fern-tree gullies, I intended to have tested for the percentage of their alkaloids prior to this evening; but the timely performance of this investigation was frustrated. I think that I have proved the hardiness or adaptability of these important plants for the warm Palm valleys of East Gipps Land, as many indigenous plants from that genial spot are quite as much, if not more, susceptible to the night-frosts of our city than the Cinchonæ, if harsh, cutting winds are kept from the latter. But as yet I am unacquainted with the likely results of remunerative Cinchona cultivation within the boundaries of this colony, as far as such depends on the constituents of the soil. That inquiries of this kind are not mere chimeras may be conceded after an explanation of this kind for the benefit of future technology. Geology, one of the brightest satellites which rotate around the sun of universal science, continues to send its lustre into the darkness which yet involves so many of the great operations in tellurian nature. Further insight into the relation of this discipline of science to vegetable physiology is certain to shed abundance of light also on many branches of applied industry. The causes why the Iron-bark trees of our auriferous quartz ridges differ so materially from the conspecific tree of alluvial flats can only be explained geologically. So it is with the narrow-leaved Eucalyptus amygdalina on open stony declivities as compared with the broad-leaved Eucalyptus fissilis, which in such gigantic dimensions towers up from our deep forest valleys. But all this has an important bearing on technological exertions in manifold directions. The timber chosen by the artisan from a wrong locality may impair the soundness of a whole building; or a factory may prove not lucrative simply because it is placed on a wrong spot for the best raw material.

A thousand of other industrial purposes might yet be served by a close knowledge of plants. So the designer might choose patterns far more beautiful from the simple and ever-perfect beauty of nature than he gains from distorted forms copied into much of our tapestry; thus a room, now-a-days, as a rule, decorated with unmeaning and often, as far as imitation of nature is concerned, impossible figures, might become, geographically or phytographically, quite instructive. If here the founders of territorial estates—some, perhaps, as large as the palatinates of the Middle Ages—should wish to perpetuate the custom of choosing a symbol for family arms, they—as the Highland clans, who adopted special plants of their native mountains for a distinguishing badge—might select, as the ancestral emblem, the flowers of our soil, destined, perhaps, to be traced, not without pride, by many a lineage through a hundred generations.

Precise knowledge of even the oceanic vegetation, in its almost infinite display of forms, offers not merely the most delicate objects for design, but brings before us its respective value for manure, or the importance of various herbage on which fishes will browse; while such marine weeds may as well be transferred from ocean to ocean, as ova of trout have been brought from the far north to these distant southern latitudes. Who could foresee when first iodine was accidentally discovered in sea-weeds, through soda factories, or bromine subsequently appeared as a mere substance of curiosity, what powerful therapeutic agents thereby were gained for medicine, what unique results they would render for chemical processes, of what incalculable advantages they would prove in physiological researches or microscopic tests; and how, without them, photographic art could not have depictured, with unerring fidelity, millions of objects, whether of landscapes or of the starry sky, whether of the beings dear to us or the relics of antiquity, whether enlarging the scope of lithography or recording the languages, which the flashing of telegraphic electricity sends to a dwelling or to an empire? Even the vegetable fossils, deep-buried in the earth or in the cleavage of rocks, when viewed by the light of phytology, become so many letters on the pages of nature's revelation, from which we are to learn the age of strata, or may trace the sources of metallic wealth, or by which we may be guided to huge remnants of forests of bygone ages, stored up for the utilization of this epoch, or may comprehend, as far as mortal understanding serves us, successive changes in tellurian creation.

When Ray and, subsequently, Jussieu, framed the first groundwork for the ordinal demarcation of plants; when Tournefort, by defining generic limits, brought further clearness into the chaos of dawning systematic knowledge, and when Linnæ gave so happily to each plant its second or specific name, but little was it indeed foreseen what a vast influence these principles of sound methodic arrangement would exercise, not only on the easy recognition of the varied forms of vegetable life, but also on the philosophic elucidation of their properties and uses, and this for all times to come. Many, even at the present day, and among them at times those on whom the destinies of whole states and populations may depend, can recognize in phytographic and other scientific labors but little else than a mere play-work; yet, without such labors, every solid basis for applying the knowledge of plants to uses of any kind would be wanting. We would stray, indeed, unguided in a labyrinth between crude masses or inordinate fragments, instead of dwelling in a grand and lasting structure of knowledge, unless science also in this direction had raised its imperishable temples. But how much patient and toilsome research had to be spent thus to bring together in a systematic arrangement all the products of this wide globe; how many dangers of exploring travelers had to be braved to amplify the material for this knowledge, and how many have to pass away, even now-a-days, persecuted and worried like Galileo at his time, no one yet has told, nor will tell. Well may we feel with the great German poet, as expressed in Bulwer Lytton's beautiful wording :

> " I will reward thee in a holier land,
> Do give to me thy youth !
> All I can grant you lies in this command—
> I heard, and trusting in a holier land,
> Gave my young joys to truth."

But is there nothing higher than the search of earthly riches, and is to this all knowledge of the earth's beautiful vegetation also to be rendered subservient ? Is there nothing loftier than to break the flowers for our gayeties or to strew them along a mirthful path ? There is ! They raised the noblest feelings of the poet at all ages ; they spoke the purest words of attachment ; they ever were the silent harbingers of love. They smilingly inspired hope anew in unmeasured sadness, and on the death-bed or at the grave they appear to link together, as symbols of ever-returning springs, the mortal world with immortality ; they ever teach us some of the sublimest revelations of our eternal God,

The laurel crown of the hero was a people's highest reward of chivalrous and glorious deeds.

The myrtle or orange-wreath for bridal curls remains the proudest gift to youthful hope.

The little blooming weed, content in a parched and dreary desert, revived the strength of many a sinking wanderer (Mungo Park); the ever unalterable beauty and harmony of moral structures preaches the truths of eternal laws in the universe — a faith that gave expression to Schiller's memorable words, as repeated by that leading British statesman, Gladstone: "It's not all chance the world obeys." The innocent loveliness of nature's flowers has often aroused anew the shaken spirit of the philosopher, and to these and other gifts of nature the American bard alludes when he speaks of the great zoologist, Agassiz, of whose friendship I may well be proud:

> "And whenever the way seemed so long,
> Or his heart began him to fail,
> She would sing a still more wondrous song,
> Or tell a more marvellous tale."

And when it seems that all hopes of the weeping mother are extinguished, or even the teachings of religion may well-nigh forsake her, then the deep meaning of some of our noblest poems, inspired by nature, is understood, and faith in eternity once more embraced.

> "And the mother gave in tear and pain
> The flowers she most did love;
> She knew she would find them all again
> In the fields of light above."

> "And with childlike credulous affection
> We behold their tender bud expand—
> Emblems of our own resurrection—
> Emblems of the bright and better land."

Eucalyptus Globulus.
(Showing the Seed Cups.)

AUSTRALIAN VEGETATION.

The great continent of Australia exhibits throughout its varied zones marked diversities in the physiognomy of its vegetation. These differences stand less in relation to geographical latitudes than to geological formations, and especially climatical conditions. Yet it is in few localities only where the peculiar features, impressed by nature as a whole on the Australian landscape, cannot at once be recognized. The occurrence of Eucalypts and simple-leaved Acacias in all regions, and the preponderance of these trees in most, suffice alone to demonstrate that in Australia we are surrounded largely by forms of the vegetable world which, as a complex, nowhere re-occur beyond its territory, unless in creations of ages passed by.

In a cursory glance at the vegetation, as intended on this occasion, it is not the object to analyze its details. In viewing vegetable life here, more particularly as the exponent of clime, or as the guide for settlement, or as the source of products for arts and manufactures, we may content ourselves by casting a view only on the leading features presented by the world of plants in this great country. While the absence of very high and wooded mountains imparts to the vegetation throughout a vast extent of Australia a degree of monotony, we perceive that the occurrence of lofty forest ranges along the whole eastern and south-eastern coast changes largely there the aspect of the country, and in this alteration the mountainous island Tasmania greatly participates. Thus the extensive umbrageous forest regions of perpetual humidity commence in the vicinity of Cape Otway; extend occasionally, but not widely interrupted, through the southern and eastern part of Victoria, and thence, especially on the seaside slopes of the ranges, throughout the whole of extra-and intra-tropical East Australia in a band of more or less width, until the cessation of elevated mountains on the northern coast confines the regions of continued moisture to a narrow strip of jungle-land margining the coast. In this vast line of elevated coast-country, extending in length over nearly three thousand miles, and which fairly may pass as the "Australian jungle," the vegetation assimilates more than elsewhere to extra-Australian types, especially to the impressive floral features of continental and insular India. Progressing from the Victorian promontories easterly, and thence northerly, we find that the Eucalypts, which still preponderate in the forest of the southern ranges, gradually forsake us, and thus in eastern Gipps Land commences the vast assemblage of varied trees which so much charms by its variety of forms, and so keenly engages attention by the multiplicity of its interest. Bathed in vapor from innumerable springs or torrents, and sheltered under the dark foliage of trees very varied in form, a magnificent display of the Fern-trees commences, for which further westerly we would seek in vain the climatic conditions. Even isolated sentries, as it were, of the Fern-tree masses are scattered not further west than to the craters of extinct volcanoes near Mount Gambier, and although colossal Todea Ferns, with stems six to ten feet high, and occasionally as thick, emerge from the streamlets which meander through the deep ravines near Mount Lofty, on St. Vincent's Gulf, we miss there the stately Palm-like grace of the Cyatheæ, Dicksoniæ, and Alsophilæ, which leave on the lover of nature who ever beheld them the remembrance of their inexpressible beauty. These Fern-trees, often twenty to thirty, occasionally fifty to seventy feet high, and at least as many years old, if not older, admit readily of removal from their still mild and humid haunts to places where, for decorative vegetation, we are able to produce the moisture and the shade necessary for their existence. Of all Fern-trees of the globe that species which predominates through the dark glens of Victoria, Tasmania, and parts of New South Wales, the Dicksonia Antarctica (although not occurring in the antarctic regions), is the most hardy and least susceptible to dry heat. This species, therefore, should be chosen for garden ornaments, or for being plunged into any park glens; and if it is considered that trees half a century old may with impunity be deprived of their foliage and sent away to distant countries as ordinary merchandise, it is also surprising that a plant so abundant has not yet become an article of more extended commerce.

A multitude of smaller ferns, many of delicate forms, are harbored under the shade of jungle vegetation, amounting in their aggregate to about one hundred and sixty species, to which number future researches in north-east Australia will undoubtedly add. The circular Asplenium nidus, or great Nest Fern, with fronds often six feet long, extends to the eastern part of Gipps Land, but the equally grand Stag-horn Fern (Platycerium alcicorne and P. grande) seemingly cease to advance south of Illawarra, while in northern Queeensland Angiopteris evecta count among the most gorgeous, and two slender Alsophilæ among the most graceful forms. The transhipment of all these Ferns offers lucrative inducements to traders with foreign countries. Epiphytal Orchids, so much in horticultural request, are less numerous in these jungle-tracts than might have been anticipated, those discovered not yet exceeding thirty in number. Their isolated outposts advance in one representative species—the Sarcochilus Gunnii—to Tasmania and the vicinity of Cape Otway, and in another—Cymbidium canaliculatum—toward Central Australia. The comparative scantiness of these epiphytes contrasts as strangely with the Indian Orchid-vegetation as with the exuberance of the lovely terrestrial co-ordinal plants throughout most parts of extra-tropical Australia, from whence one hundred and twenty well-defined species are known. Still more remarkable is the almost total absence of Orchids, both terrestrial and epiphytal, from north and north-west Australia, an absence for which in the central parts of the continent aridity sufficiently accounts, but for which we have no other explanation in the north than that the species have as yet there effected but a limited migration. To the jungles and cedar-brushes—the latter so named because they yield that furniture-wood so famed as the Red Cedar (Cedrela taona, a tree identical as a species with the Indian plant, though slightly different in its wood) are absolutely confined the Anonaceæ, Laurineæ, Monimieæ, Meliaceæ, Rubiaceæ, Myrsineæ, Sapoteæ, Ebenaceæ, and Anacardieæ, together with the Baccate Myrtaceæ, and nearly all the trees of Euphorbiaceæ, Rutaceæ, Apocyneæ, Celastrineæ, Sapindaceæ, which, while often outnumbering the interspersed Eucalypts, seem to transfer the observer to Indian regions. None in the multitude of trees of these orders, with exception of our tonic-aromatic Sassafras-tree (Atherospermum moschatum) and Hedycarpa Cunninghami, which supplies to the natives the friction-wood for igniting, transgress in the south the meridians of Gipps Land. Palms cease also there to exist, but their number increases northward along the east coast, while in Victoria these noble plants have their only representative in the tall-cabbage or Fan-palm of the Snowy River — that Palm which, with the equally hardy Areca sapida of New Zealand, ought to be established wherever the Date is planted for embellishment. Rotang Palms (Calami of several species) render some of the northern thickets almost inapproachable, while there, also, on a few spots of the coast, the Cocoanut-tree occurs spontaneously. A few peculiar Palms occur in the Cassowary country, near Cape York, and others around the Gulf of Carpentaria, as far west as Arnhemsland. The tallest of all, the lofty Alexandra Palm (Ptychosperma Alexdræ), extends southward to the tropic of Capricorn, and elevates its majestic crown widely beyond the ordinary trees of the jungle. The products of these entire forests is as varied as the vegetation which constitutes them. As yet, however, their treasures have been but scantily subjected to the test of the physician, the manufacturer, or the artisan. The bark of Alstonia constricta, like that of allied Indian species, is ascertained to be febrifugal, so that of Chionanthus axillaris, and Brucea Sumatrana. Caoutchouc might be produced from various trees, especially the tall kinds of Ficus. The lustre and tint of the polished woods of others is unrivaled. Edible fruits are yielded by Achras Australis, Achras Pohlmaniana, Mimusops kauki, Zizyphus jujuba, Citrus Australis, Citrus Planchonii, Eugenia Myrtifolia, Eugenia tierneyana, Parinarium nonda, the Candlenut-tree (Aleurites triloba), and the cluster Fig-tree (Ficus vesca, which produces its bunches from the stem); also by species of Owenia and Spondias, and by several brambles and vines. Starchy aliment or edible tubers are furnished by Tacca pinnatifida, by several Cissi (C. opaca, C. clematidea, acrid when unprepared), Marsdeni viridiflora, Colocasia antiquorum, Alocasia macrorrhiza, by a colossal Cycas, some Zamiæ, and several kinds of Yam (Dioscorea bulbifera, Dioscorea punctata, and other species). Backhousia citriodora and Myrtus fragrantissima yield a cosmetic oil; so, also, Eucalyptus citriodora, a tree not confined to the jungle, and two kinds of Ocimum. Semecarpus anacardium, the marking Nut-tree, is a native of the most northern brush-country. The medicinal Mallotus Philippinensis, and the poisonous Excæcaria Agallocha are more frequent. Baloghia lucida furnishes a red dye never to be obliterated.

Many of the trees of the coast-forests of East Australia range from the extreme north to the remotest south, among them the Palm-panax; others, like Araucaria Cunninghami, extend only to the northern part of New South Wales, while some, including Araucaria Bidwelli, or the Bunya-Bunya-tree, so remarkable for its large, edible, nutlike seeds, and the Australian Kauri, Dammara robusta, are confined to very circumscribed or solitary areas. The absence of superior spice-plants (as far as hitherto ascertained) amidst a vegetation of prevailing Indian type is not a little remarkable, for Cinnamomum Laubatii ranks only as a noble timber-tree, and the native nutmegs are inert. The scantiness of acanthaceous plants is also a noticeable fact. Podostemoneæ have not yet been found. Many plants of great interest to the phytographer are seemingly never quitting the north-eastern peninsula; among these the Banksian banana (Musa Banksii), the pitcher-plant (Nepenthes Kennedyana), the vermillion-flowered Eugenia Wilsonii, the curious Helmholtzia acorifolia, the Mar shal-tree, Archidendron Vaillantii (the only plant of the vast order of Leguminosæ with numerous styles), the splendid Diplanthera quadrifolia, Ficus magnifolia, with leaves two feet long, the tall Cardwellia sublimis, and the splendid Cryptocarpa Mackinnoniana, are especially remarkable. Rhapidophara, Pothos, Piper, together with a host of Lianes, especially gay through the prevalence of Ipomæas, tend with so many other plants to impart to the jungle part of Australia all the luxuriance of tropical vegetation. Of the two great Nettle-trees, the Laportea gigas occurs in the most northern regions, while Laportea photinifolia is more widely diffused. Helicia is represented by a number of fine trees far south, some bearing edible nuts. Doryanthes excelsa, the tall spear-lily, is confined to the forests of New South Wales. The flowers of Oberonia palmicola are more minute than those of any other orchideous plant, although more than two thousand species are known from various parts of the globe. The display of trees eligible for avenues from these jungles is large. The tall Fern-palm (Zamia Denisonii), one of the most stately members of the varied Australian vegetation, is widely, but nowhere copiously, diffused along the east coast; it yields a kind of sago, like allied plants. The beans of Castanospermum Australe, which are rich in starch, and those of Entada pursætha, from a pod often four feet long, are, with very many other vegetable substances, on which Mons. Thozet has shed much light, converted by the aborigines into food.

If plants representing the genera Berberis, Impatiens, Rosa, Begonia, Ilex, Rhododendron, Vaccinium, or, perhaps, even Firs, Cypresses, and Oaks, do at all occur in Australia, as in the middle regions of the mountains of India, it will be on the highest hills of north-east Australia — namely, on the Bellenden Ker ranges, mountains still unapproachable through the hostility of the natives—where they will find the cooler and simultaneously moist tropical climate congenial to their existence. But whatever may be the variety and wealth of the primitive flora of East Australia, it is only by the active intelligence and exertions of man that the greatest riches can be wrought from the soil. Whatever plants he may choose to raise—whatever costly spices, luscious fruits, expensive dyes; whether cacao, manihot, or other alimentary plants; whether sugar, coffee, or any others of more extensive tropical tillage—for all may be found wide tracts fitted for their new home.

The close access to harbors facilitates culture, while the expansive extent of geographical latitude on the east coast admits of choosing such spots as in each instance present the most favorable climatic conditions for the success of each special plantation. Beyond the coast ranges the country westward changes with augmenting dryness generally at once into more open pastoral ground. Basaltic downs and gentle verdant rises of eminent richness of herbage may alternately give way to Brigalow scrubs, or sandstone plateaux, or porphyritic or granitic hills, and with the change of the geological formation a change, often very apparent, will take place also in the vegetation. Inland we will lose sight of the glossy, dense, umbrageous foliage, which now only borders a generally low coast in the north, terminating there frequently in mangroves. Strychnos nux vomica occurs among the coast-bushes here, and also an Antiaris (A. macrophylla); but whether the latter shares the deadly poison of the Upas-tree of Java and Sumatra requires to be ascertained. Tamarindus Indica is known from Arnhemsland, and the French bean (Phaseolus vulgaris) in a spontaneous state from the north-west coast. Eucalypts, again, form away from the sea the prevailing timber, but with the exception of the Red Gum-tree (Eucalyptus rostrata), which lines most of the rivers of the whole of the Australian interior, the southern species are replaced by others, never of gigantic growth, in some instances adorned with brilliant scarlet or crimson blossoms. But neither these nor many distinct kinds of northern Acacias and Melaleucas stamp on the country the expression of peculiarity. Familiar Australian forms usually surround us, though those of the cooler zone, and even the otherwise almost universal Senecios, are generally absent. Cyperus vaginatus, perhaps the best of all textile rushes, ranges from the remotest south to these northern regions. Hibiscus tiliaceus, with other malvaceous plants, is here chosen by the natives for the fibre of their fishing-nets and cordage. An occasional interspersion of the dazzling Erythrina vespertilio, of Bauhinia Leichardti, Erythrophlæum Laboucheri, Livistonia Palms, and many Terminaliæ, some with edible fruits, Cochlospermum Gregorii, C. heteronemum, remind, however, of the flora of tropical latitudes, which, moreover, to the eye of an experienced observer, is revealed also in a multitude of smaller plants, either identical with South Asiatic species or representing in peculiar forms tropical genera. The identity of about six hundred Asiatic plants (some cosmopolitan) with native Australian species, has been placed beyond doubt, and to this series of absolutely identical forms, as well derived from the jungle as from grounds free of forest, unquestionably several hundred will yet be added.

Melaleuca leucadendron, the Cajeput-tree of India, is among Indo-Australian trees one of the most universal; it extends, as one of the largest timber-trees of north Australia, along many of its rivers, and in diminutive size over the dry sand-stone table-lands. The Asiatic and Pacific Casuarina equisetifolia accompanies it often in the vicinity of the coast. By far the most remarkable form in the vegetation of north-west Australia is the Gouty-stem-tree (Adansonia Gregorii); but it is restricted to a limited tract of coast-country. It assumes precisely the bulky form of its only congener, the Monkey-bread-tree, or Baobab of tropical Africa (Adansonia digitata), dissimilar mainly in having its nuts not suspended on long fruit-stalks. Evidence, though not conclusive, gained in Australia, when applied to the African Baobab, renders it improbable that the age of any individual tree now in existence dates from remote antiquity. This view is also held by Dr. G. Bennett, of Sydney. The tree is of economic importance ; its stem yields a mucilage indurating to a tragacanth-like gum. It is also one of the few trees which introduces the unwonted sight of deciduous foliage into the evergreen Australian vegetation. Numerous swamps and smaller lakes exist within moderate distance of the coast ; as in many other parts of Australia, these waters are surrounded by the wiry Polygonum (Muehlenbeckia Cunninghami), and in Arnhemsland occasionally also by rice-plants, not distinct from the ancient culture-plant. But here, in almost equinoctial latitudes, the stagnant fresh waters are almost invariably nourishing two Water-lilies of great beauty (Nymphæa stellata and Nymphæa gigantea), which give, by the gay display of their blue, pink, or crimson shades of flowers, or by their pure white, a brilliant aspect to these lakes ; and even the Pythagorean bean (Nelumbo nucifera) sends occasionally its fine shield-like leaves and large blossom and esculent fruits out of the still and sheltered waters. But how much could this splendor of lake-vegetation be augmented if the reginal Victoria, the prodigious Water-lily of the Amazon River, was scattered and naturalized in these lakes, to expand over their surface its stupendous leaves, and to send forth its huge, snowy, and crimson, fragrant flowers,

It would add to the aliment which the natives now obtain from these lakes and swamps by diving for the roots and fruits of the Nymphæ, or for the tubers of Heleocharis sphacelata, of species of Aponogeton, or by uprooting the starchy rhizomes of Typha augustifolia (the Bullrush), when eager of adding a vegetable compound to their diet of Unio shells, or of water-fowls and fishes, all abounding on these favorite places of their resort. Trapa bispinosa, already living, like the Victoria, in the tanks of our conservatories, ought, with Trapa natans, for the sake of its nuts, not only to be naturalized in the waters of the north, but also in the lagoons and swamps of the south. Around these lakes Screw-Pines (Pandanus spiralis and Pandanus aquaticus) may often be seen to emerge from the banks, the latter, as recorded already by Leichhardt, always indicative of permanent water. The young top-parts of the stems of these Pandans, when subjected to boiling, become free of acridity, and thus available, in cases of emergency, for food. Opilia amentacea and the weeping Eugenia eucalyptoides, together with a native cucumber (Cucumis jucunda), are here among the few plants yielding edible fruit. Purslane (Portulaca oleracea) abounds, and in sandy soil it is found pleasantly acidulous. It will always be acceptable, as a salad or spinach, especially in affections from scurvy, and its amylaceous seeds might, in cases of distress, be readily gathered for food. A delicious tall perennial spinach (Chenopodium auricamum) is not unfrequent. Beyond one kind of Sandarach Callitris no Pines exist in the north, except the Araucaria Greyi, noticed on a circumscribed spot on the Glenelg river. The true Bamboo (Bambusa arundinacea) lines, as far as yet discovered, only the banks of a few of the rivers of Arnhems-land.

To the pastoral settler, for whom more particularly the generally open Eucalyptus country or the treeless or partly scrubby tracts are eligible, it must be of significance that the rainfall occurs with frequency during the hottest part of the year. Hence, during the Summer, grass and herbage is pushing forth with extraordinary rapidity and exuberance, while a judicious burning at the cooler season, together with the effect of regular dews, is certain to produce fresh forage during the dryer months. An almost endless variety of perennial nutritious grasses, allied to Indian species, or even identical with them, are known to exist. The basaltic downs of the north and north-west produce almost precisely the same vegetation which has rendered Darling and Peak Downs so famed in the east. This almost absolute identity of plants is a sufficient indication of great semblance of climate, for which the rise of the country, though one not very considerable, to some extent may account. On the ranges which divide the waters of the east coast from those of Carpentaria the vine luxuriates; its fruit, indeed, suffers occasionally from frost.

How far the tract south of the more littoral northern country may continue to bear prevailingly the features of fertility cannot be predicated. There can be no greater fallacy than to prejudge an untraversed country—a fallacy to which explorers are prone, and which, in some instances, has retarded advancement of geographical discoveries and of new locations of permanent abodes, while, in other instances, it has led to disastrous consequences. A country should be judged with caution. Even from elevations comparatively inconsiderable, as such nearly always proved away from the eastern coast, the orb of vision is limited. A traveler may, buoyant with hope, commence his new daily conquest on the delightful natural lawns or the verdant slopes of a trap formation; and, before many hours' ride, he may, to his dismay, be brought without water to a bivouac between the sand-waves of decomposed barren rocks. But as suddenly a few hours' perseverance may bring him again into geological regions of fertility when he least expected it; smiling landscapes may again burst into his view, and he may establish his next camp on limpid water, sufficient for the requirements of a future city. The nature of a country is not ruled by climate and latitude alone, but quite as much, if not more, by its geological structure. Glancing on the map of an unexplored country, we are apt to take in our conjectures the former alone for a guide, until the latter, by actual field-operations, becomes our stronghold in topographical mapping. It would thus be unsafe to assume that the great western half of the interior consists mainly of desolate, uninhabitable desert-country, or even to contend that the reappearance on Termination Lake, or on the Murchison river, of so very many of the plants which give to the saltbush country, or the Mallee and Brigalow scrubs, on the extensive depression of the Darling system, their physiognomy, necessitates their uninterrupted extension from the rear of Arnhems-land to the Murray Desert, or to Shark Bay. From demonstrating-facts like these we dare no more infer but that likely many similar tracts of flat country are stretching over portions of the wide intervening spaces. But who will predict more? May not the large system of salt lakes formed by the drainage of rain into cavities of saline flats be found limited to the less distant portions of the interior of Western Australia, and may it not thus, by a gradual rise of the ground (evidently manifest northerly), give place to a system of fresh-water lakes or lagoons, or even of such springs as rewarded the exertions of the keenly-searching explorers west of Lake Eyre? And although it must be admitted that no ranges simultaneously lofty and wooded, and thus originating springs and rivulets for the formation of larger rivers, are likely to exist to any extent in the extra-tropical part of the western interior, because such rivers have not found their way to the coast; yet it is still possible, and rather probable, that mountains as high, and much less bare than Gawler Range, and even much more extensive, may give rise to interior water-courses, along which the dwellings of new colonists may be established, and to which our pasture-animals may flock, but which, in their sluggish progress, cannot force their way to the ocean, and are thus lost in numerous more or less ample inland basins. Years hence, on even less-favored spots, artesian borings may afford the means of stay for a dense population, should, as may be anticipated, mineral riches prove to be scattered not merely over the vicinity of the west coast and Spencer's Gulf, but also over interjacent areas of geological similarity. York's Peninsula, close to settlements, was long left an uninhabited and desolate spot until its richness of copper-ore was disclosed. So other unmapped parts of Australia are also likely to prove rich; and, although equal facilities for the transit of the mineral treasures would not always exist, its discovery would be certain to lead to the occupation of the country and to the extension of pastoral colonization, until an increasing population and augmented conveniences for traffic could turn mineral wealth, however distantly located, advantageously to account. But how vastly might not any barren tracts of the interior be improved, and how many a lordly possession be founded, by patient industry and intelligent judgment! Storage of water, raising of woods, dissemination of perennial fodder-plants, will create alone marvellous changes; and for these operations means are readily enough at command. Even the scattering of the grains of the common British Orache (Atriplex patulum), an annual but autumnal plant, would, on the barest ground, realize fodder for sheep; and the number of plants which for such purpose could be chosen are legion. The storage of rain-water might, in any rising valley, be so effected as to render it, simply by gravitation, available for irrigating purposes.

As a curious fact, it may be instanced that, in some of the waterless sandy regions of South Africa, the copious naturalization of melon-plants has afforded the means of establishing halting-places in a desert country. On the sandy shores of the Great Bight, and also anywhere in the dry interior, such plants might be easily established. The avidity with which the natives at Escape Cliffs preserved the melon-seeds, after they once had recognized the value of their new treasure, holds out the prospect of the gradual diffusion of such vegetable boons over much unsettled country.

No part of Australia has the marked peculiarities of its vegetation so strongly expressed, and no part of this great country produces so rich an assemblage of species within a limited area as the remotest south-western portion of the continent. Indeed, the southern extremity of Africa is the only part of the globe in which an equally varied display of vegetable forms is found within equally narrow precincts, and endowed also with an equal richness of endemic genera. It is beyond the scope of this brief treatise to enter fully into a detailed exposition of the constituents of the south-western flora. It may mainly suffice to view such of the vegetable products as are drawn already into industrial use, or are likely to be of avail for the purpose. Foremost in this respect stands, perhaps, the Mahogany-Eucalypt (Eucalyptus marginata). The timber of this tree exhibits the wonderful quality of being absolutely impervious to the inroads of the limnoria, the teredo, and chelura—those minute marine creatures so destructive to wharves, jetties, and any work of naval architecture exposed to the water of the sea; it equally resists the attacks of termites. In these properties the Red Gum-tree of our own country largely shares. The Mahogany-Eucalypt has, in the Botanic Gardens of this city, been brought for the first time largely under cultivation, and as, clearly, the natural supply of this important timber will, sooner or later, prove inadequate to the demanded requirements, it must be regarded as a wise measure of the governments of France and Italy now to establish this tree on the Mediterranean shores—a measure for which still greater facilities are here locally offered.

The Tuart (Eucalyptus gomphocephala) is another of the famed artisan's woods of south-western Australia. The Karri (Eucalyptus colossea or diversicolor) attains, in favorable spots, a height of four hundred feet. Eucalyptus megacarpa constitutes the Blue Gum-tree, which rivals that of Tasmania and Victoria in size, but is otherwise very distinct. Its timber, as well as that of the Tuart, on account of their hardness, are employed for tramways and other works of durability. The fragrant wood of several species of Santalum forms an article of commercial export. Some kinds of Casuarina, quite peculiar to that part of Australia, furnish superior wood for shingles and for a variety of implements. Several species of Acacia, especially Acacia acuminata, the raspberry-scented Wattle, equally restricted to the south-west coast, yield fragrant and remarkably solid wood and a pure gum. To this part of Australia was naturally also restricted the Acacia lophantha, which has, for the sake of its easy and rapid growth and its umbrageous foliage, assumed such importance, even beyond Australia, for temporary shelter-plantations. Many other products, such as gum-resins, sandarach, tanner's bark, all of great excellence, are largely available; but these substances show considerable similarity to those obtained in other Australian colonies.

The extraordinary abundance, however, of the Xanthorrhœas through most parts of the south-west territory gives special interest to the fact (1845) promulgated by Stenhouse, that anthrazotic, or nitro-picric acid—a costly dye—may, with great ease and little cost, be prepared from the resin of these plants. Indeed, this is the richest source for this acid, the resin yielding half its weight in dye. Fiber of great excellence and strength is obtained from the bark of Pimelea clavata, a bush widely distributed there. It resembles that of bast from Pimelea axiflora in Gipps Land, and that from Pimelea microcephala of the Murray and Darling desert. A Fern-palm (Zamia Fraseri) attains in West Australia a height of fifteen feet. It is there, like some congeners of America and South Africa, occasionally sacrificed for the manufacture of a peculiar starch, though the export of the stems (and perhaps of those of the Xanthorrhœas also) would prove much more profitable, inasmuch as these, when deprived of their noble crown of leaves, though not of their roots, will endure a passage of many months, even should the plants be half a century old. Such any wool-vessel might commodiously take to Europe. This alimentary Fern-palm, well appreciated by the aborigines for the sake of its nuts, together with a true kind of Yam (Dioscorea hastifolia), the only plant on which the natives, in their pristine state, anywhere in Australia, bestowed a crude cultivation, are, with species of Borya, Sowerbæa, Hæmodorum, Ricinocarpus, Macarthuria, Chloanthes, Aphanopetalum, Xylomelum, Caleana, Calectasia, Petrophila, Leschenaultia, Pseudanthus, Nematolepis, Nuytsia (the terrestrial mistletoe), Leucolæna, Commersonia, Rulingia, Keraudrenia, Mirbelia, Gastrolobium, Labichea, Melichrus, Monotaxis, Actinotus, and Stypandra, remarkable for their geographical distribution; because, as far as we are hitherto aware, these West Australian genera have no representatives in the wide interjacent space until we approach toward the eastern, or, in a few instances, to the northern regions of Australia, Zamia alone having been noticed in South Australia (Zamia Macdonnellii), but there as an exceedingly local plant. Neither climate nor geologic considerations explain this curious fact of phytogeography. Over some of the healthy tracts of scrub-country, toward the south-west coast, poisonous species of Gastrolobium (Gastrol bilobum, G. oxylobioides, G. calycinum, G. callistachys) are dispersed. These plants have, in some localities, rendered the occupation of country for pastoral pursuits impossible, but these poison-plants are mostly confined to barren spots, and it is not unlikely that, by repeated burnings, and by the raising of perennial fodder-plants, they could be suppressed, and finally extirpated. Fortunately, in no other parts of Australia Gastrolobium occurs, except on the inland tract from Attack Creek to the Suttor River, where flocks must be guarded against access to the scrub-patches harboring the only tropical species (Gastrolobium grandiflorum). The deadly effect occasionally produced by Lotus Australis, a herb with us of very wide distribution, and extending also to New Caledonia, and the cerebral derangements manifested by pasture animals, which feed on the Darling River pea (Swainsona Greyana), need yet extensive investigation, but may find their explanation in the fact that the organic poisonous principle is only locally, under conditions yet obscure, developed ; or in the probable circumstance that, like in a few other leguminous plants, the deleterious properties are strongly concentrated in the seed. The gorgeous desert-pea (Clianthus Dampierii), which, in its capricious distribution, has been traced sparingly from the Lachlan River to the north-west coast, offers still to seed-collectors a lucrative gain.

A prominent aspect in the vegetation of south-west Australia emanates from the comparatively large number of singularly beautiful Banksia-tree, preponderant there as the arborous Grevilleæ in North Australia. The existence of but two of that genus, Banksia Australis, and B. ornata, in the extensive tract of interior and coast land, from the head of the Australian Bight, to the vicinity of Port Philip, renders the occurrence of an increased number of trees of this kind in East Australia again still more odd. Rutaceous and goodeniaceous plants, though in no part of the Australian continent rare, attain in the south-west their greatest numerical development, and should not be passed silently, or, like Epacrideæ, as merely ornamental plants, though still so rare in our gardens; but these elegant plants deserve also attention for their diaphoretic properties, or for the bitter tonic principle which pervades nearly all the species of the two orders. Stylideæ are here still more numerous than in our north, and comprise forms of great neatness; while sundews (Droseræ) are also found to be more frequently than in anyo ther part of Australia, and indeed of the globe. When, glittering in their adamantine dew, they reappear as the harbingers of Spring from year to year, they are greeted always anew with admiration. But the greatest charm of the vegetation consists in the hundreds of myrtaceous bushes peculiar to the west, all full of aromatic oil; among these again, the feather-flowered numerous Verticordiæ, the crimson Calothamni, and the healthy Calythrices vie with each other as ornaments. Still also of this order many gorgeous plants exist in other parts of, especially extra-tropical Australia. The numerous bushes of Leguminosæ, and Proteacæ, in south-west Australia, are also charming. The introduction of all these into European conservatories might be made the object of profitable employment. Annual herbs of extreme minuteness, belonging chiefly to Compositæ, Umbelliferæ, Stylideæ, and Centrolepideæ, are here, as in other parts of extra-tropical Australia, in their aggregate more numerous than minute phanerogamic plants in any other part of the globe. A line of demarcation for including the main mass of the south-west Australian vegetation may almost be drawn from the Murchison River, or Shark Bay, to the western extremity of the Great Bight; because to these points penetrates the usual interior vegetation, which thence ranges to Sturt's Creek, to the Burdekin, Darling, and Murray rivers, while the special south-west Australian flora ceases to exist as a whole beyond the limits indicated.

The marine flora of south-west Australia is likewise eminently prolific in specific forms, perhaps more so than that of any other shore. Many of the algæ are endemic, others extend along the whole southern coast and Tasmania, where again a host of species proved peculiar; some are also extra-Australian. The whole eastern coast contrarily, and also the northern and the north-western, with the exception of a few isolated spots, such as Albany Island, contrast with the southern coast as singularly poor in algæ. In a work exclusively devoted to the elucidation of the marine plants of Australia—a work which as an ornament of phytographic literature stands unsurpassed, and which necessitated lengthened laborious researches of its illustrious author, the late Professor Harvey, here on the spot—the specific limits of not less than eight hundred algæ are fixed. Some of these are not without their particular uses. A few yield caragaheen, all bromine and iodine. Macrocystis pyrifera, the great kelp, which may be seen floating in large masses outside Port Philip Heads, attains the almost incredible length of many hundred feet, while a single plant of the leathery, broad Urvillea potatorum constitutes a heavy load for a pack-horse.

The wide, depressed interior, once supposed to be an untraversable desert, consists, as far as hitherto ascertained, much less of sandy ridges than of subsaline or grassy flats, largely interspersed with tracts of scrub, and occasionally broken by comparatively timberless ranges. The great genus Acacia, which gives to Australia alone about three hundred species (and, therefore, specific forms twice as numerous as that of any Australian generic type), sends its shrubs and trees also in masses over this part of the country, where, with their harsh and hard foliage, they are well capable to resist the effect of the high temperature during the season of aridity, while they are equally contented with the low degree of warmth to which, during nights of the cool season, the dry atmosphere becomes reduced. Handsome bushes of Eremophila, with blossoms of manifold hue, decorate the scrubs throughout the whole explored interior. Among the desert Cassiæ two simple-leaved kinds are remarkable. Of the Acaciæ, none here, except A. Farnesiana, have pinnated leaves, and even one is leafless ; the pinnated Acaciæ being restricted to the more littoral tracts, and even there from the Great Bight to Guichen Bay entirely absent. If shelter plantations of the rapidly-growing Eucalypts, Acacias, and Casuarinas were raised, a vast variety of useful plants could be reared along the water-courses of the more central parts of Australia. Saltbushes, in great variety, stretch far inland, and this is the forage on which flocks so admirably thrive. Probably the extensive Asiatic steppes have to boast of no greater diversity of salsolaceous plants than our own. Nevertheless, even here much could be added to the productiveness of these pasturages by the introduction of other perennial fodder herbs. Grasses, wherever they occur, are varied, and a large share is perennial, nutritious, and widely diffused. As corroborative, it may be instanced that Anthistiria ciliata, the common kangaroo-grass, almost universally ranges over Australia, and thus also over the central steppes of the continent. It extends, indeed, to Asia and North Africa also. Besides, through the interior, grasses, especially of Panicum and Andropogon, are numerous, either on the oases, or interspersed with shrubs on barren spots. Festuca or Triodia irritans, the porcupine-grass of the settlers, is restricted to the sands of the extra-tropical latitudes; Festuca or Triodia viscida, chiefly to the sandstone table-lands of the tropics.

Only in the south-eastern parts of the continent, and in Tasmania, are the mountains rising to alpine elevations. Mount Hotham, in Victoria, and Mount Kosciusko, in New South Wales, form the culminating points, each slightly exceeding seven thousand feet in height. In the ravines of these summits lodge perennial glaciers; at six thousand feet snow remains unmelted for nearly the whole of the year, and snow-storms may occur in these elevations during the midst of Summer. At five thousand feet the vegetation of shrubs generally commences, and up to this height ascend two Eucalypts, Eucalyptus coriaceæ and Gunnii, forming dense and extensive thickets; E. coriaceæ assuming, however, in lower valleys, huge dimensions. Both these, with most of our alpine plants, would deserve transplanting to middle Europe, and to other countries of the temperate zone, where they would well cope with the vicissitudes of the climate. In Tasmania, the Winter snow-line sinks considerably lower, and in its moister clime many alpine plants descend there along the torrents and rivulets to the base of the mountains which here are constantly clinging to cold elevations. Mount William is the only sub-alpine height isolated in Victoria from the great complex of snowy mountains, but it produces, beyond Eucalyptus alpina, and Pultenæa rosea, which are confined to the crest of that royal mountain, only Celmisia longifolia and little else as the mark of an alpine or rather subalpine flora. Celmisia also is one of the few representatives of cold heights in the Blue Mountains; and from New England we know only Scleranthus biflorus, a cushion-like plant, exquisitely adapted for margining garden plots, and Gualtheria hispida, as generally indicating spots on which snow lodges for some of the Winter months. The mountains of Queensland would need in their tropical latitudes a greater height than they possess for nourishing analogous forms of life, but the truly alpine vegetation of the high mountains of Tasmania contrasts in some important respects with that of the Australian Alps — namely, therein that under the prevalence of a much higher degree of humidity, plants which delight to be bathed in clouds, or in the dense vapors of the surrounding Fern-tree valleys, are much more universal; and that the number of peculiar alpine genera is much greater than here. Thus, while in Tasmania the magnificent Evergreen Beech (Fagus Cunninghami) covers many of the ranges up to sub-alpine rises, it predominates as a forest-tree in Victoria only at the remotest sources of the Yarra, the Latrobe, and the Goulburn rivers, and on Mount Baw-Baw. To this outpost of the Australian Alps (now so accessible to metropolitan tourists) are restricted also several plants, such as Oxalis Magellanica and Libertia Lawrencii, which are almost universal on all the higher hills of Tasmania. Fagus Cunninghami, though descending into our Fern-tree ravines, transgresses nowhere the Victorian land-boundaries, but a noble fagus-forest, constituted by a distinct and equally evergreen species, Fagus Moorei, crowns the high ranges on which the Bellinger and M'Leay rivers rise. This, however, the snowy mountains of Tasmania and of continental Australia have in common, that the majority of the alpine plants are not representing genera peculiar to colder countries, but exhibit hardy forms, referable to endemic Australian genera, or such as are allied to them. So, as already remarked, we possess alpine species, even of Eucalyptus and of Acacia, besides of hibbertia, oxylobium, bossiæa, pultenæa, eriostemon, boronia didiscus, epacris, leucopogon, prostanthera, grevillea, hakea, persoonia, pimelea, kunzea, baeckea, stackhousia, mitrasacme, xanthosia, coprosma, velleya, prasophyllum; yet anemone, caltha, antennaria, gaultheria, alchemilla, seseli, œnothera, huanaca, abrotanella, ligusticum, astelia, gunnera, and other northern or western types, are not altogether missing, though nowhere else to be found in Australia but in glacial regions.

About half a hundred of the highland plants are strictly peculiar to Victoria; the rest prove mainly identical with Tasmanian species; but a few of ours, not growing in the smaller sister-land, are, strange as it may appear, absolutely conspecific with European forms. Rather more than one hundred of the lowland plants ascend, however, to the glacial regions; some of these are simultaneously desert-species.

The only genus of plants absolutely peculiar to the Victorian territory, Wittsteinia, occurs as a dwarf subalpine plant, of more herbaceous than woody growth, restricted to the summits of Mount Baw-Baw; this, moreover, remained hitherto the only representative of vaccinieæ in all Australia; it produces, like most of the order, edible berries.

The verdant Summer-herbage of valleys, which snow covers during the Winter months, will render with increasing value of land-estates these free, airy, and still retreats in time fully occupied as pasturage during the warmer part of the year. Here, in sheltered glens, we have the means of raising all the plants delighting in the coolest clime. Rye-culture could probably be carried on at considerable elevation.

Of all the phanerogamic plants of Tasmania, about one hundred and thirty are endemic; of those about eighty are limited to alpine elevations, or descend from thence only into cool, umbrageous valleys. The generic types peculiar to the island are again almost all alpine (milligania, campynema, hewardia, pterygopappus, tetracarpæa, anodopetalum, cystanthe, prionotis, microcachrys, diselma, athrotaxis, pherosphæra, bellendena, cenarrhenes, archeria), only acradenia and agastachys belonging seemingly to the lowlands, but show at once a fondness for a wet, insular clime. The few Tasmanian genera, represented besides only in Victoria, are richea, diplarrhena, drymophila, juncella. In the Tasmanian highlands flora endemic shrubby asters and epacrideæ, and the singular endemic pines of various genera, constitute a marked feature. A closer and more extended inquiry into the geological relation of great assemblages of vegetation will shed probably more light on the enigmatic laws by which the dispersion of plants is ruled. Australian forms predominate also in Tasmania, at snowy heights, so Eucalyptus gunnii, E. coccifera, and E. urnigera. The famous Huon-pine (Dacrydium Franklini), the Palmheath (Richea pandanifolia), the celery-topped pine (Phyllocladus rhomboidalis), and the deciduous beech (Fagus Gunnii) are among the most striking objects of its insular vegetation. Mosses, lichenastra, lichens, and conspicuous fungs abound both in alpine and low regions ; indeed, cryptogamic plants, except Algs and microscopic fungs, are nowhere in Australia really frequent except in Tasmania, in the Australian Alps, and in the Fern-tree glens of Victoria and part of New South Wales. The Musk-tree (Aster argophyllus) of Tasmania and south-east Australia is the largest of the few trees produced by the vast order of compositæ in any part of the globe, while Prostanthera lasianthos, its companion, exhibits the only real tree known in the extensive family of

Labiatæ. The almost exclusive occupation of vast littoral tracts of Gippsland, and some of the adjoining islands, by the dwarf Xanthorrhœa minor, is remarkable. Mistletoes do not extend to Tasmania, though over every other part of Australia; neither the Nardoo (Marsilea quadrifolia), of melancholic celebrity, though to be found in every part of the continent, and abounding in innumerable varieties throughout the depressed parts of the interior. Equisetaceæ occur nowhere. The total of the species to be admitted as well-defined, and hitherto known, from all parts of Australia, approaches (with exclusion of microscopic fungi) to ten thousand.

It has been deemed of sufficient importance to append to this brief memoir an index of all the trees hitherto discovered in any part of Australia.* Such statistics lead to reflection and comparison. They also bring more prominently before the contemplative mind the real access which in any branch of special knowledge may have been obtained. In this instance it is the only table with which this document has been burdened, though kindred lists might have readily been elaborated. Nor would this imperfect sketch of Australian vegetation have been extended to any detailed enumerations whatever did not the trees impress on the vegetation of each country its most distinctive feature, and had we not learned how great a treasure each land possesses in its timber—whether as raw product to artisans or as objects of therapeutic application, whether as material for the products of manifold factories or as the source of educts in the chemical laboratory; whether as the means of affording employment to the workman, or even as the me-

* Index omitted.

dium for regulating the climate. May we revert only to the circumstance, as elucidating the great physiographic characters of countries and their mutual relation, that notwithstanding the close proximity of New Zealand, *none* of its trees (though very many of its herbs) are positively identical with any observed in Australia; and yet, hundreds of ours can in no way be distinguished from Indian trees. Moreover, in a philosophical contemplation of the nature of any country and the history of its creation, our attention is likely to be in the first instance engaged in a survey of the constituents of its pristine forests, and greatly is it to be feared that in ages hence, when much of the woods will have sunk under ruthless axes, the deductions of advanced knowledge thereon will have to be based solely on evidence early placed on record.

The marvellous height of some of the Australian, and especially Victorian trees, has become the subject of closer investigation since, of late, particularly through the miners' tracks, easier access has been afforded to the back-gullies of our mountain system. Some astounding *data*, supported by *actual* measurements, are now on record. The highest tree previously known was a Karri - Eucalyptus (Eucalyptus colossea), measured by Mr. Pemberton Walcott, in one of the delightful glens of the Warren River of western Australia, where it rises to approximately four hundred feet high. Into the hollow trunk of this Karri three riders, with an additional pack-horse, could enter and turn in it without dismounting. On the desire of the writer of these pages, Mr. D. Boyle measured a fallen tree of Eucalyptus amygdalina, in the deep recesses of Dandenong, and obtained for it the length of four hundred and twenty feet, with proportions of width, indicated in a design of a monumental structure placed in the Exhibition ; while Mr. G. Klein took the measurement of a Eucalyptus on the Black Spur, ten miles distant from Healesville, four hundred and eighty feet high! Mr. E. B. Heyne obtained at Dandenong as measurements of height of a tree of Eucalyptus amygdalina: Length of stem from the base to the first branch, two hundred and ninety-five feet; diameter of the stem at the first branch, four feet; length of stem from first branch to where its top portion was broken off, seventy feet; diameter of the stem where broken off, three feet; total length of stem up to place of fracture, three hundred and sixty-five feet; girth of stem three feet from the surface, forty-one feet. A still thicker tree measured, three feet from the base, fifty-three feet in circumference. Mr. George W. Robinson ascertained, in the back-ranges of Berwick, the circumference of a tree of Eucalyptus amygdalina to be eighty-one feet at a distance of four feet from the ground, and supposes this Eucalypt, toward the sources of the Yarra and Latrobe rivers, to attain a height of half a thousand feet. The same gentleman found Fagus Cunninghami to gain a height of two hundred feet and a circumference of twenty-three feet.

It is not at all likely that in these isolated inquiries chance has led to the really highest trees, which the most secluded and the least accessible spots may still conceal. It seems, however, almost beyond dispute, that the trees of Australia rival in length, though evidently not in thickness, even the renowned forest-giants of California, Sequoia Wellingtonia, the highest of which, as far as the writer is aware, rise in their favorite haunts at the Sierra Nevada to about four hundred and fifty feet. Still, one of the mammoth trees measured, it is said, at an estimated height of three hundred feet, eighteen feet in diameter! Thus to Victorian trees for elevation the palm must apparently be conceded. A standard of comparison we possess in the spire of the Munster of Strasbourg, the highest of any cathedral of the globe, which sends its lofty pinnacle to the height of four hundred and forty-six feet, or in the great pyramid of Cheops, four hundred and eighty feet high, which, if raised in our ranges, would be overshadowed probably by Eucalyptus-trees.

The enormous height attained by not isolated, but vast masses of our timber-trees in the rich diluvial deposits of sheltered depressions within Victorian ranges, finds its principal explanation, perhaps, in the circumstance that the richness of the soil is combined with humid geniality of the climate, never sinking to the colder temperature of Tasmania, nor rising to a warmth less favorable to the strong development of these trees in New South Wales, nor ever reduced to that comparative dryness of air which even to some extent, in the mountain-ravines of South Australia, is experienced. The absence of living gigantic forms of animal life amidst these the hugest forms of the vegetable world is all the more striking.

Statistics of actual measurement of trees compiled in various parts of the globe would be replete with deep interest, not merely to science, but disclose also, in copious instances, magnitudes of resources but little understood up to the present day. Not merely, however, in their stupendous altitude, but also in their celerity of growth, we have, in all probability, to accede to Australian trees the prize. Extensive comparisons instituted in the Botanic Garden of this metropolis prove several species of Eucalyptus, more particularly Eucalyptus globulus, and Ecalyptus obliqua, as well as certain Acacias — for instance, Acacia decurrens, or Acacia mollissima—far excelling in their ratio of development any extra-Australian trees, even on dry and exposed spots, such into which spontaneously our Blue Gum-tree would not penetrate. This marvellous quickness of growth, combined with a perfect fitness to resist drought, has rendered many of our trees famed abroad, especially so in countries where the supply of fuel or of hard woods is not readily attainable, or where for raising shelter, like around the Cinchona-plantations of India, the early and copious command of tall vegetation is of imperative importance. To us here this ought to be a subject of manifold significance. I scarcely need refer to the fact that for numerous unemployed the gathering of Eucalyptus-seeds, of which a pound weight suffices to raise many thousand trees, might be a source of lucrative and extensive employment; but on this I wish to dwell: that in Australian vegetation we probably possess the means of obliterating the rainless zone of the globe, to spread at last woods over our deserts, and thereby to mitigate the distressing drought, and to annihilate, perhaps, even that occasionally excessive dry heat evolved by the sun's rays from the naked ground throughout extensive regions of the interior, and wafted with the current of air to the east and south—miseries from which the prevalence of sea-breezes renders the more littoral tracts of West and North Australia almost free. But in the economy of nature the trees, beyond affording shade and shelter, and retaining humidity to the soil, serve other great purposes. Trees, ever active in sending their roots to the depths, draw unceasingly from below the surface-strata those mineral elements of vegetable nutrition on which the life of plants absolutely depends, and which, with every dropping leaf, is left as a storage of aliment for the subsequent vegetation. How much lasting good could not be effected, then, by mere scattering of seeds of our drought-resisting Acacias, and Eucalypts, and Casuarinas, at the termination of the hot season along any water-course, or even along the crevices of rocks, or over bare sands or hard clays, after refreshing showers? Even the rugged escarpments of the desolate ranges of Tunis, Algiers, and Morocco might become wooded; even the Sahara itself, if it could not be conquered and rendered habitable, might have the extent of its oases vastly augmented; fertility might be secured again to the Holy Land, and rain to the Asiatic plateau, or the desert of Atacama, or timber and fuel be furnished to Natal and La Plata. An experiment instituted on a bare ridge near our metropolis demonstrates what may be done.

Not Australia alone, but some other countries, have judiciously taken advantage of the facilities afforded by Australian tree-vegetation for raising woods—an object which throughout the interior might be initiated by rendering this an additional purpose of the expeditions to be maintained in the field for territorial and physiographical exploration; and more, it might deserve the reflection of the Legislature, which allots to the pastoral tenants their expansive tracts of country, whether or not along with squatting pursuits—indeed, for the actual benefit of the pastoral occupant himself the inexpensive first steps for general forest-culture in the woodless regions should be commenced.

Within the ranges which produce these colossal trees but few habitations exist; indeed, we might traverse a line of a thousand miles as yet without a dwelling. The clime is salubrious; within the sheltered glens it cannot in excellence be surpassed. Hot winds, from which our exposed plains, as well as any rises of northern and western aspect, so much suffer, never reach the still and mild vales of the forests; frosts are only experienced in the higher regions. Speaking of Victoria especially, it is safe to assert that there alone many thousand square miles of mountainous country, timbered with Stringy-bark trees (Eucalyptus obliqua) are as yet lying dormant for any other but isolated mining operations. And yet, might not families which desire to strike out a path of independent prosperity, which seek a simple patriarchal life in a salubrious locality of seclusion, and which command the needful strength of labor within their own circle, choose these happy glens as their permanent abodes? Though the timbered rises of the ranges may be as yet unlucrative for cultivation, or even be sterile, the valleys are generally rich, irrigated by clear brooks, and spacious enough for isolated homes, and the limited number of pasture animals pertaining to them. The costlier products of culture might be realized, especially so in the Fern-tree glens; tea, and possibly cinchona, and coffee also ; so, lucrative fibres, dye-plants of easy growth and simple preparation, as instanced by grass-cloth, or madder ; or medicinal plants, such as senna, and various herbs, or, perhaps, even the Erythroxylon coca, a plant of almost fabulous properties. Or should the settler prefer, beyond raising the simple requirements for his rural life, to devote his attention solely to the gain which the surrounding timber treasuries are certain to offer, he will find ample scope for his energy and industry. The Eucalypts, as now proved by extensive and accurate experiments, will yield him tar in abundance ; they will furnish fibres, even those of Stringy-bark as one of the cheapest and most extensively available paper material. By a few simple appliances he may secure, simultaneously with the tar, also wood-vinegar and wood-spirit; and these again might locally be at once converted into dye materials and varnishes. He might obtain potash from woods, and volatile oils from the leaves of Eucalypts in almost any quantity, by artless processes and with scarcely any cost. He might gather the gum-resins and barks for either medicinal or tanning purposes, or he might effect a trade in Fern-trees ; he might shake the Eucalyptus grains out of their capsules, and might secure locally other mercantile substances far too numerous to be enumerated here. Whoever may choose these ranges as a permanent home, and may direct thoughtfully his attention to the future, will recognize that the mere scattering of the acorns of the Cork-tree or the seeds of the Red Cedar over cleared and yet sheltered ground, or the planting of the vine and olive, will yield to his descendants sources of great riches.

In closing these concise and somewhat chaotic suggestions, which scarcely admit of methodical arrangement, unless by expansion into the chapters of a volume, we may—indulging in a train of thought—pass from special to general considerations.

Belgium, one of the most densely populated of all countries, and yet one of the most prosperous, nourished within an area less than one half that of Tasmania a population three times exceeding that of all the Australian colonies; yet one fifth of the Belgian territory consists of forests. Not to any considerable extent smaller than Europe, our continent is likely to support in ages hence a greater population; because, while here no frigid zone excludes any portion of the territory from productiveness, or reduces it anywhere to very circumscribed limits, it embraces a wide tropical tract, destined to yield us products nowhere to be raised under the European sky. The comparatively unbroken uniformity of vast tracts of Australia certainly restricts us for the magnificent sceneries and the bracing air of the countries of our youth here to the hilly coast-tracts; but still we have not to endure the protracted colds of middle and northern European Winters, nor to contend with the climatic difficulties which beset tillage operations or pastoral pursuits, and which, by patient perseverance, could not be removed or be materially lessened.

While we are deprived of advantages so pleasing and so important as those of large river communications, we enjoy great facilities for land traffic, facilities to which every new discovery of coal-layers will add.

Judicious forest culture, appropriate to each zone, will vastly ameliorate the clime, and provide for the dense location of our race ; for transplanting of almost every commodity, both of the vegetable and animal empire, we possess, from the Alps to the Steppes, from the cool mountain forests to the tropic jungles, conditions and ample space.

River-waters, now flowing unutilized to the ocean, when cast over the back plains, and artesian borings also, will effect marvellous changes. Steam power and the increased ingenuity of machinery applied to cultivation will render the virgin soil extensively productive with far less toil than in older countries, while the teachings of science will guard us against the rapacious systems of culture and the waste of fertilizers which well-nigh involved ruin to many a land. Of ferocious land animals Australia is free. We have neither to encounter extensive hordes of savages to dispute the possession of the soil, nor the still more dangerous opposition of half-civilized barbarians, such as for ages yet may obstruct the progress of civilization in the great interior of Africa.

Our continent, it may be foretold prophetically, will ere long be regarded of so high a territorial value that *no* tract, however much disregarded now, will remain unoccupied. Our continent, surrounded moreover by the natural boundaries of three oceans, free and unconnected, must advance, by extraneous influences undisturbed, by ancient usages unretarded, to that greatness to which British sovereignty will ever give a firm stability.

FIFTH

ANNUAL CATALOGUE

OF THE

Santa Barbara College

Santa Barbara, California.

Board of Directors.

1875-6.

COL. W. W. HOLLISTER,
ELLWOOD COOPER,
CHAS. FERNALD,
JOHN P. STEARNS,
JOHN EDWARDS,
CHARLES E. HUSE,
F. W. FROST,
WILLIAM M. EDDY,
T. WALLACE MORE,
G. P. TEBBETTS.

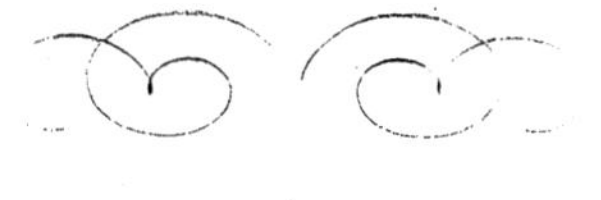

Officers and Committees.

1875-6

ELLWOOD COOPER.

Treasurer.

F. W. FROST.

G. P. TEBBETTS.

Finance and Building Committee.

CHAS. FERNALD, CHARLES E. HUSE,
J. P. STEARNS, JOHN EDWARDS,
G. P. TEBBETTS.

Executive Committee.

ELLWOOD COOPER, T. WALLACE MORE,
Col. W. W. HOLLISTER, F. W. FROST,
WILLIAM M. EDDY.

Board of Instructors.

PRINCIPAL.

ELLWOOD COOPER.

ASSOCIATE PRINCIPAL.

MRS. ELLWOOD COOPER.

TEACHERS.

PROF. A. NEUMEYER, MISS LUCY E. WHITTON,
PROF. C. H. SILLIMAN, MISS L. K. PERSHING,
PROF. ALPHONSE BEL, MISS KATE BRONSON,
PROF. M. J. GORDON, MISS S. L. ANDERSON.

Students

OF THE

Santa Barbara College,

1875-76.

LIST OF PUPILS.

ACADEMIC COURSE.

Ayers, Jennie
Bailard, Theresa E.
Bailard, John
Barnard, Frank E.
Barnard, Nellie D.
Barham, John H.
Borrowe, Fannie
Bowers, Anna A.
Bowers, Demoss
Bowers, John
Brastow, George B.
Bradbury, Nora A.
Bronson, Lulu
Bronson, Kate
Casebeere, Isbella
Castinos, Albert
Cook, Fairie
Cook, Nina
Cooper Ellen
Cooper, Fannie
Conant, Mrs. T. S.
Des Granges, Otto
Dimmick, Walter
Dugdale, Horace C.
Dunne, James C.
Duval, Charles S.
Edwards, Anna
Edwards, Charles
Elwell, Frank
Fernald, Beatrice
Franklin, Anabel E.
Franklin, Mrs.
Frost, Clarinda
Gibbs, Annie
Gibbs, George
Gibbs, Laura W.
Gibbs, Lausian
Gibbs, Mrs. E. H.
Greenwell, Arty C.
Greenwell, Charles B.
Goss, Josephine
Hampton, Fannie

Hampton, Pallie
Hampton, Jeff.
Harrison, James K.
Haight, Charles B.
Harford, Freddie
Hatch, Mrs.
Hawley, Ernest S.
Hawley, Lilian
Hawley, Jessie R.
[illegible]
Hayne, Bennie
Hayne, Alston
[illegible]
Higgins, Fred. L.
Hill, Jessie
Huse, Alice R.
Johnson, Mackey
Kalisher, Fannie
Knapp, Sadia R.
Lake, George B.
Lake, Winnie
Low, Fannie
Lucas, Hattie M.
Mayhew, Jennie
McLaren, Anna
McLaren, Jennie
More, Belle
More, Mary
More, Wallace
More, Alex. S.
More, Willie
Newmayer, Bene
Newmayer, Bismarck
Newmayer, Lillie
Newmayer, Walter
Norway, William R.

Olsen, Fred.
Olsen, Minnie
Pacheco, John
Perkins, Allie T.
Perkins, Grace F.
Perkins, Isabel D.
Perkins, May W.
Perin, Edith
Pierce, Charles D.
[illegible]
Riggen, William
Safford, Morton
Sawtelle, Vivian F.
Shaw, James B.
Skeels, Katie
Skeels, William
Smith, De Witt
Snodgrass, David C.
Stearns, Edith
Steel, John Jay
Steel, Willie
Stevens, Albert B.
Stoddard, Harrie
Stone, George Fred.
Stone, Luella
Tallant, Lucy
Tebbetts, Horace B.
Tebbetts, John E.
Tebbetts, Mollie V.
Tryce, James
Upson, Grace
Walcott, Earle A.
Walcott, Mabel
Walcott, Maude
Weldon, Jennie
Wright, Sallie

The Foundation.

Under the laws of California, in the year 1869, the College of Santa Barbara was incorporated. It owes its origin to the feeling that, with its health-giving breezes and almost perfect climate, southern California is destined to be the Paradise of America, and that consequently a necessity exists for an educational institution which shall carry its pupils further than is the province of the public schools. The citizens of Santa Barbara and vicinity felt that the rapidly-increasing population and wealth of their own county and those adjoining would justify considerable expense in providing for their children better means and methods of education. In obedience to this feeling, a number of public-spirited citizens of Santa Barbara organized a stock company, who erected suitable buildings for the immediate wants. The success attained by their first efforts, and the encouragement of almost the entire community, induced the incorporators to re-organize under the new Code, with a capital stock of *One Hundred Thousand Dollars.*

The institution is governed by a Board of eleven Directors, who have been chosen from among the most prominent and intelligent citizens of the county. They serve only in order to promote the educational interest of the State, and to open wider fields of learning for the sons and daughters of the country. Their best thoughts are given to the Institution.

Location.

Santa Barbara, the seat of the college, lies on the coast, two hundred and ninety miles south of San Francisco. Situated to the south of the Santa Inez mountains, it is sheltered from the coast winds. The cool and invigorating sea-breeze renders the climate mild and even. All fruits common to temperate and semi-tropical climates grow luxuriantly in its vicinity. Frosts seldom come, and Winter is a word scarcely found in the language of its people. From January to January the trees are covered with leaves and the fields are green with the revolution of crops. The fevers often found in other localities of the same latitude are never experienced. The climate is very beneficial in cases of consumption and all pulmonary diseases. The advantages of its climate are so widely admitted that people from all parts of the country are coming to make it their home. To no other locality can the parent send his child and be so assured that in every respect the climate is any nearer perfection.

Character of the Institution.

Directors and Faculty of Instruction pledge themselves to do all in their power to make the Santa Barbara College absolutely, not relatively, a good institution; to requite the trust which the people place in them with the best possible instruction; and to cultivate among all their pupils true manliness and true womanliness.

"Our plans of education are disposed to include all that the Past has handed down of good, all that the Future may offer to us. By the study of Language, Philosophy, and History, we inherit the rich experiences of Humanity; by the study of Natural Science we search after the Laws of Creation, and reach out for the Divine."

Regular attendance and punctuality at all recitations and exercises will be demanded. It will be impossible for any pupil who does not attend to his entire duty and is not prompt at every exercise to long remain in the Institution and retain his class rank. Each recitation is a link in a chain. The loss of one lesson destroys the unity of all lessons given upon the same subject. All knowledge afterward obtained is incomplete. By absence or tardiness, the pupil not only injures himself, but impedes the entire class with which he is associated. The others must wait while the subject is again explained to him. No pupil will be permitted to thus do himself and others injustice.

It is our aim not to burden students with arbitrary rules and useless restraints. Students will be given all liberty consistent with their own welfare. The government is intended to be liberal but firm in character. It will be advisory rather than compulsory. We believe that he who teaches one to govern himself is a better teacher than he who governs a score by compulsion.

The institution will be entirely free from sectarian bias. The pure morality and piety of the Scriptures, excluding everything sectarian and denominational, is the foundation of all moral and religious teachings,

The patrons, stockholders, and directors are members of every sect and denomination. Justice to them demands the utmost liberality. The Sabbath will be observed as a day of rest and religious teaching, and should be made the pleasantest of the week. Attendance upon Divine worship is expected, and parents are requested to signify the church which they prefer their children shall attend. An instructor will accompany the younger pupils.

All classes are to be frequently visited by an examining committee, whose duty it will be to see that they are making commendable progress, and report to the Board of Directors. It is requested that parents having children in the institution, or contemplating putting children under its charge, visit the classrooms, and then consult with the Principal with regard to the progress made or desired.

The College receives pupils of both sexes. It thus places itself in accord with the progressive spirit and the necessities of the West. Girls and boys have each an equal share in the instruction, and will be treated alike.

Special Features.

The points in which Santa Barbara College differs from most other educational institutions of a similar general character may be briefly summed as follows :

1. Special attention is given to Physical Culture. Recognizing the great fundamental fact that a sound mind cannot exist without a sound body, we have given much thought to the physical development of those intrusted to us.

The best gymnasium in the State, the only one connected with a school in California, is now completed and fitted up with all the apparatus necessary for practicing both heavy and light gymnastics. Every pupil will have an opportunity daily to take part in the exercises. Physiological laws will be our guide in directing them. Parents should encourage their children to be earnest in these pursuits; for in this way alone can the young be given sound bodies to supply vigor to inquiring minds. Disciplined thus in body, young men and young women will leave our institution better fitted to use that knowledge which they have acquired, both for their own good and for the good of the community.

2. The Modern Languages will receive special attention. The benefits arising from a study of the Modern Languages, both in respect to discipline and practical value, are so many and so well known that a list of them here is unnecessary. Those who desire will be offered an opportunity constantly to converse in French, German, and Spanish.

3. Vocal music will be taught every pupil. Instrumental music will receive special attention. All who have thought upon the subject acknowledge the refining influence which music has upon the individual. It also affords measureless comfort and enjoyment to the home circle. We need not assure parents that this important branch of study will always be superintended by a teacher of much experience and culture.

4. Every pupil will be instructed in the rudiments of Drawing. By no other method is a pupil taught so well to observe minutely and attentively the phenomena of nature as by a course of instruction in the art of Drawing. If any one doubts this, let him sit

down and attempt to put upon paper the simplest object within sight. He will be skeptical no longer. Drawing is but an attempt to reproduce what we see, and is the test of the accuracy of our observation and comparison.

General Statement.

The Santa Barbara College contains eight departments, with six grades in each.

1st. Mathematics.
2d. Natural Sciences.
3d. English.
4th. History and Geography.
5th. Modern Languages.
6th. Ancient Languages.
7th. Drawing and Painting.
8th. Vocal and Instrumental Music.

The classes are: The Elementary, Preparatory, First Year, Second Year, Junior Year, and Senior Year.

Course of Study.

ELEMENTARY CLASS.

First Term.

Arithmetic, Robinson's Rudiments.
Geography, Guyot's Primary.
English, Swinton's Language Primer.
Penmanship, Payson, Dunton and Scribner's No. 3.
Reading, Bancroft's Fourth Reader.
Drawing, Knudsen's first year's instruction in drawing.
Spelling, Swinton's Word Book to Lesson 106.
Music, Vocal and Instrumental.
French, Oral Exercises.
German, Ahn's Rudiments of the German Language.
Spanish, Oral Exercises.

Second Term.

Arithmetic, Robinson's Rudiments.
History, Swinton's First Lessons.
English, Swinton's Language Primer.
Reading, Bancroft's Fourth Reader.
Penmanship, No. 4.
Spelling, Swinton's Word Book to end of first year's work.

Drawing, Conclusion of first year's instruction.

Music, Vocal and Instrumental.

French, Ahn's first Primer.

German, Ahn's Rudiments continued.

Spanish, Oral Exercises continued; first lessons in reading.

Science, Hotze's First Lessons.

PREPARATORY CLASS.

First Term.

Arithmetic, Robinson's Practical and Intellectual.

Geography, Guyot's Elementary.

English, Swinton's Language Lessons.

Reading, Bancroft's Fifth Reader.

Penmanship, No. 5.

Spelling, Swinton's Word Book, second year's work to lesson 106.

Drawing, Second year's instruction in drawing.

Music, Vocal and Instrumental.

French, Ahn's first course.

German, Ahn's Method of learning the German language to ex. 60.

Spanish, Elements of Grammar.

Science, Youman's Botany.

Second Term.

Arithmetic, Robinson's Practical and Intellectual.

History, Higginson's United States.

English, Swinton's Language Lessons.

Penmanship, No. 6.

Reading, Bancroft's Fifth Reader.

Drawing, Conclusion of second year's instruction.

Spelling, Swinton's Word Book to end of second year's work.

Music, Vocal and Instrumental.

French, Ahn's first course concluded; colloquial exercises.

German, Ahn's Method continued.

Spanish, Spelling; colloquial exercises.

Science, Morse's Zoology.

FIRST YEAR.

First Term.

Arithmetic, Robinson's Practical and Intellectual.

Geography, Guyot's Intermediate.

English, Swinton's Progressive Grammar.

Penmanship, No. 7.

Spelling, Swinton's Word Analysis, begun.

Drawing, Third year's instruction in drawing.

Music, Vocal and Instrumental.

French, Ahn's second course; verbs.

Spanish, Ahn's Grammar.

German, Otto's Grammar.

Science, Physiology.

Second Term.

Arithmetic, Robinson's Practical and Intellectual, completed.

History, History of England.

English, Swinton's School Composition.

Penmanship, No. 8.

Spelling, Swinton's Word Analysis, completed.

Drawing, Conclusion of Third year's instruction.

Music, Vocal and Instrumental.

French, Ahn's Second Course concluded; Hachette's First Reader; irregular verbs.

German, Otto's Grammar; exercises in composition.

Spanish, Ahn's Grammar, continued; irregular verbs; First Reader of Mantilla.

Science, Introduction to Geology (Dana).

SECOND YEAR.

FIRST TERM.

Mathematics, Robinson's Higher Arithmetic, and Elementary Algebra.

Geography, Guyot's Common School.

English Composition and Rhetoric, Word Analysis.

Penmanship, No. 9.

Drawing, Crayon drawing.

Spelling, McElligott's Manual.

Music, Vocal and Instrumental.

French, Fasquelle's Grammar; First Reader concluded.

German, Exercises in writing German; translation.

Spanish, De Torno's combined Grammar; Second Reader of Mantilla; elements of composition.

Science, Gray's Botany.

Latin, Harkness' Latin Grammar and Reader.

Greek, Goodwin's Greek Grammar and Leighton's Reader.

SECOND TERM.

Mathematics, Robinson's Higher Arithmetic and Elementary Algebra, completed.

History, Swinton's Outlines.

English, Composition and Rhetoric, Word Analysis.

Penmanship, No. 10.

Drawing, Crayon drawing concluded.

Spelling, McElligott's Manual.

Music, Vocal and Instrumental.

French, Fasquelle's Grammar continued; Elements of Composition; Reading of Guillaume Tell (Lamartine).

German, Petermann's First Lesebuch.

Spanish, De Torno's Grammar continued; Roemer's Reader; Conversation.

Science, Chemistry.

Latin, Harkness' Introduction to Latin Composition; Cæsar's Commentaries, books I. and II.

Greek, Jones's or Arnold's Exercises; Xenophon's Anabasis begun.

JUNIOR YEAR.

First Term.

Mathematics, Robinson's University Algebra to Equations; Davies' Geometry, books I., II. and III.

History, Guizot's History of Civilization.

English, Underwood's British Authors.

Music, Vocal and Instrumental.

Spelling, Study of Words.

French, Composition; Grammar continued; Lallemagne (Mad. de Stael).

German, Whitney's Grammar and Exercises.

Spanish, Ollendorf's Grammar; Introduction to Spanish classics.

Science, Quackenboss' Natural Philosophy.

Latin, Csæar's Commentaries, books III. and IV.; Cicero's Orations against Cataline.

Greek, Boise's First Greek Lessons; Anabasis.

SECOND TERM.

Mathematics, Robinson's University Algebra to Series. Davies' Geometry, books IV., V. and VI.

History, Hopkins' American Ideas.

English, Underwood's American Authors.

Music, Vocal and Instrumental.

Spelling, Study of Words.

French, Correspondence; Conversation; Introduction to Classics.

German, Goethe's Hermann and Dorothea.

Spanish, Correspondence; Conversations; Classics.

Science, Mineralogy, lectures.

Latin, Cicero de Amicitia; Æneid.

Greek, First three books of the Anabasis completed. Smith's History of Greece.

SENIOR YEAR.

FIRST TERM.

Mathematics, Davies' Geometry, and Robinson's University Algebra completed.

History, Ancient History.

English, Elements of Criticism.

Music, Vocal and Instrumental.

Spelling, Words and their Uses, by Richard Grant Whits.

French, Grammaire complete de Poitevin; Composition; French Classics.

German, Lessing.

Spanish, Gramatica de la Academia; Conversation; Composition.

Science, Guyot's Physical Geography.

Latin, First Six Books of the Æneid completed.

Greek, Homer's Iliad, three books; Prosody.

SECOND TERM.

Mathematics, Davies' Trigonometry and Mensuration.

History, Lord's Modern History.

English, Elements of Criticism.

Music, Vocal and Instrumental.

French, Grammaire de Poite vin, concluded ; Modern Literature ; Conversation ; Philology of the French language.

German, Goethe's Faust.

Spanish, Modern Literature of Spain and South America compared.

Science, Burritt's Geography of the Heavens.

Latin, Odes of Horace.

Greek, Iliad continued.

OPTIONAL STUDIES.

Book-keeping, Single and Double Entry.

Instrumental Music, Piano and Violin.

Special Singing Lessons.

Painting and Special Drawing.

The grade of each pupil is determined at the time of admission, by a careful examination in his or her previous studies; and at the close of each subsequent term the pupil is advanced to the next higher grade, provided that on examination he or she is found qualified.

The lack of thoroughness in the elementary branches on the part of the older pupils who enter the college—indeed, the almost total neglect of training in these important steps of education, makes it necessary for us to advise those who are looking forward to placing their children under the care of this institution to see that this elementary work be carefully looked after, so that when these same children enter they may be able to grade with pupils who have come up through the different classes of this school.

To accommodate those who may wish to have their children's education begin in this school, we have established, in connection with it, a KINDERGARTEN on the most improved plan.

TIME-TABLE—SANTA BARBARA COLLEGE.

Period Begins.	Mathematics.	Natural Sciences.	English.	History and Geography.	Ancient and Mod. Languages.	Drawing and Penmanship.
9:00 A.M.	Sr.	E.	P.	F.	S.	J.
9:45 "	J.	Sr.	E.	P.	F.	S.
10:30 "	S.	J.	Sr.	E.	P.	F.
11:15 "	F.	S.	J.	Sr.	E.	P.
2:00 P.M.	P.	F.	S.	J.	Sr.	E.
2:45 "	E.	P.	F.	S.	J.	Sr.
3:30 "	B.	......	......	....	....	....

School opens at 8:45 A. M., fifteen minutes being occupied in the morning exercises. The school-day is divided into seven recitation periods, with five-minute recess between each recitation. Drawing will alternate with writing, and reading with vocal music. In the table, Sr. stands for Senior Class; J, Junior Class; S, Second Year Class; F, First Year Class; P, Preparatory Class; E, Elementary Class; and B, for Book-keeping.

Miscellaneous.

Expenses.

DAY PUPILS.

Kindergarten course, board, lights, washing, and tuition in all studies (excepting those under the head of extra charges), per term of five months	$140
Elementary course	150
Preparatory course, with first, second, junior and senior years	175

Where two children occupy the same sleeping-room a deduction per term of $12.50 each will be made.

EXTRA CHARGES.

Piano or Violin Lessons, each	5 00	per month.
Special Singing Lessons	5 00	" "
Painting and Special Drawing	5 00	" "
Book-keeping	2 00	" "
When more than one modern language is taken, an extra charge will be made of	5 00	" "

Books and stationery for the use of pupils are furnished free of charge. They must, however, be kept in perfect order, and be returned to the school. All ABUSED *articles will be charged. Books should be covered.*

Pupils, in addition to their ordinary wearing apparel and toilet articles, will be require dto furnish nothing but a pair of heavy colored blankets. Each article of apparel must be marked with the pupil's name in full; otherwise the laundry cannot be responsible.

CALENDER YEAR—1876-77.

Begins.....................................August 1st, 1876.
Ends...May 24th, 1877.

VACATION.

Begins.................................December 15th, 1876.
Ends.....................................January 8th, 1877.

GENERAL REMARKS.

Pupils will not be received in the *Boarding Department* unless they can furnish satisfactory evidence of good moral character, and give sufficient security for the prompt payment of their bills.

Any donations to the cabinets or library will be gladly received.

All possible care will be taken of pupils who may become sick. Parents may rest assured they will be early informed of any illness on the part of their children.

A variety of good and wholesome food will be put upon the table, and every means adopted to remove the common prejudice against the board supplied by educational institutions.

Simplicity in dress is suggested. No uniform has been deemed advisable, but, in order better to perform the various exercises in gymnastics, A LOOSE ATTIRE IS ESSENTIAL.

All bills payable at the end of every four weeks.

Pupils are requested to make no presents to teachers. It is hard to accept, still harder to refuse.

Pupils guilty of habitual disorder, insubordination, or immorality, will be sent before the Board of Directors.

The only acceptable excuse for absence or tardiness is sickness or unavoidable prevention.

REGULATIONS FOR BOARDING PUPILS.

Rising bell.........at 7 o'clock Dinner..........at 12:30 P. M.
Breakfast.............at 7:45 Supper.............at 6 P. M.
Retiring bell....................................at 9 P. M.

Each pupil, on entering the college, obtains a copy of the Rules to be observed, and a Time-table showing how he or she is employed every hour daily.

To the Teachers.

First. You should be well qualified. You should have the knowledge of the science, which you can acquire by close application only, under an able teacher, for a considerable length of time.

Second. Secure the confidence and respect of your class by thorough teaching and a gentlemanly deportment on *all* occasions.

Third. Strive to have your class make the degree of advancement which will recommend you to to the public as an *able* teacher.

Fourth. Stand or sit before your class, place your eyes upon the whole, and give special attention to him who is the process of analysis.

Fifth. Give each member of the class the amount of time for the examination of his subject which his peculiar structure of mind may require.

Sixth. Never drill your class unless *you* have the page in which you are exercising them.

Seventh. Allow no time to elapse between the *pupil's* error and *your* correction.

Eighth. Do not interrupt the process of analysis with a *long explanation.* Say *wrong, sir,* or *wrong.* Utter these words the very *moment* in which he commits the error.

Ninth. You should speak with propriety. You should set an example which your pupils may safely follow.

Tenth. Do not play with your *knife,* with your *ruler,* with your *walking-stick,* with your *book,* with your *pencil,* with your *watch-chain,* with your fingers, etc., etc., while you are teaching. No man of sound mind will ever waste his time in the practice of these *dandy* tricks.

Eleventh. You should not permit your pupils to indulge in any of the above crazy feats. Pupils are much disposed to be shaking their feet, thumping the books and tables with their fingers, twisting and turning their persons; these are pranks which modest persons will never play off upon themselves or others. All buffoonery, debasing jests, scurrility, and low mirth are entirely destructive to anything like progress; and all who indulge in them, whether young or old, rich or poor, should be cut off from the class at once.

Twelfth. You should not permit one pupil to teach another while *you* are giving instructions. Each member should listen to the teacher.

Thirteenth. Devote all your spare hours to the study of valuable books; acquire all the information which your health and opportunities will permit. The more knowledge you have the better you can teach. Never slight the poor, nor flatter the rich; view all as the children of *one* Father. Do all the good you can, and prevent all the harm in your power.

Fourteenth. The teachers will be held responsible for the books, pens, pencils, rubbers, rulers, and ink-wells belonging to the several departments over which they preside; also for the defacing of desks, walls, or black-boards.

To The Students.

" *On Study.* Sit down to your studies every day under the deep impression that what you have to do demands your best powers and your utmost diligence. Strive to acquire the habit of close and fixed attention in study. He who has not learned the art of fastening his mind on the subject, and of holding that subject strictly and firmly before it, will never look deeply into anything; will never accomplish anything which deserves the name of investigation.

Constantly implore the aid of the Holy Spirit in study. The duty of humbly and importunately asking the blessed Spirit's influence to sanctify our affections, and to aid us in cultivating all the graces and virtues of the Christian life, will not, I suppose, be disputed by any one who has the smallest tincture of piety. Never imagine that any valuable amount of knowledge, and especially of accurate knowledge, is to be obtained without labor. Leave nothing till you have done it well. Skimming over the surface of any subject is of little use. Passing on to something else before that which precedes is half understood is really oftentimes worse than useless. Bring your acquaintance with any subject to the test of writing. It is wonderful how far the crudeness and inadequacy of a man's knowledge, on a given subject, may be hidden from his own mind, until he attempts to express what he knows on paper. He then finds himself at a loss at every step, and cannot proceed without much extension, and no less correction of his former attainments. Carefully maintain order in study. He who does not study upon a plan will never pursue his studies to much advantage. Be a close student through life.

A good scholar. It is found to be a great deal easier to become a good scholar than an indifferent one. He who studies everything thoroughly, to which he turns his attention, doubles his power at almost every step. All men, whether they understand the philosophy of language or not, judge, and generally very correctly, of the improvements of any man's mind by the ease with which they understand what he proposes to communicate. There can be no accurate thinking, and of course no correct reasoning, without a precise and correct use of words.

Rules.

1. Every pupil must conform in all respects to the regulations of the College.

2. Pupils late, and those returning after absence, must, before joining their classes, present a written excuse, signed by parent or guardian.

3. When the College-bell rings, every pupil is at

once to go to his class-room, and take his place quietly and orderly, having all necessary books, pencils, etc., etc.

4. When the lesson is finished, every pupil is to leave the class-room quietly and orderly; and all shouting, pushing, running, and boisterous behaviour about class-room doors at the hours of meeting, changing or dismissal of classes, are strictly prohibited.

5. No playing or jumping over forms or desks is allowed in any class-room at any time.

6. When dismissed, each boy or girl is at once to proceed to the play-ground, or go home. Loitering in or about class-rooms is strictly prohibited.

7. All school-books must be covered and kept as clean as possible; and no writing on or destroying books will be permitted.

8. No school-books are to be left lying about any of the class-rooms or College premises.

9. No pupil is permitted to destroy or injure pens, desks, maps, windows, or any College property whatever; all such damages to be repaired at the expense of the defaulter.

10. No pupil is permitted to cut or write upon the desks, offices, walls, boards, fences, or other College furniture or property.

11. Throwing stones or other missiles within the College grounds, or in the roads or streets adjoining, is strictly prohibited.

12. When a pupil accidentally or otherwise breaks a window, or injures College property, he must immediately report it to the officer on duty.

13. No waste paper is to be thrown about class-rooms, premises, or play-ground, but into "the waste-paper box."

14. Every pupil must carefully prepare all lessons prescribed; and no excuse will be sustained for non-preparation, except a written one from a parent or guardian.

15. Quiet, order, decorum, and gentlemanly conduct must be strictly observed at all times.

16. Every pupil must be respectful and obedient to masters. Any marks of disrespect or impertinence in word or manner will be summarily punished.

17. The use of all improper language is strictly prohibited; and any pupil who persists in it, after having been warned, will be expelled from the College.

Rules for Boarding Pupils.

1. The use of *tobacco* POSITIVELY FORBIDDEN. Under no circumstances will a boy be allowed to use tobacco in any form.

2. Boys will be allowed to ramble on the hills on Saturdays, also to take early morning walks; but no boy, *young* or *old*, will be allowed to go *down town* unless accompanied by a teacher.

3. Not more than two boys will occupy the same sleeping-room, and no visiting in each other's rooms will be permitted unless by special permission from a teacher and for a special purpose. No jumping on beds or romping of any kind is allowed in bed-rooms.

4. Boys who rise early, and before the rising-bell, must wear slippers so as not to disturb the household or those who desire rest.

5. Boys are required to keep their rooms in perfect order and appear at the table with hair and clothes brushed, boots blacked and nails cleaned, and must bathe every week.

6. Girls will not be allowed to go outside the College grounds unless accompanied with a teacher. Pupils will be encouraged to walk out every day at four, when the day's exercises are over. A teacher will always be in readiness to go with them.

7. Girls will be expected to make their own beds, and to keep their rooms in perfect order.

8. No pupil, either *boy* or *girl*, will be allowed to visit friends of their parents, unless under the supervision of a teacher, as they might make acquaintances whose company may retard the progress in their studies.

9. Pupils who do not receive instruction in instrumental music will not be allowed to use the pianos. Those receiving instruction will have a fixed time for practice, and no disturbance by the presence of other pupils during the practice periods will be permitted. It has been found that indifferent thumping for mere pastime is detrimental to progress. All pianos will be closed when not required for schedule use.

10. Pupils will not be permitted to attend theatres, entertainments, or places of amusement of any kind, neither to go out in the evenings. On Sunday evenings, from 7 to 8, instruction will be given in Bible History.

11. Perfect silence must prevail in the buildings after 9:15 P. M.

To Parents.

The Rules and Regulations have been inserted that parents may know just what is expected of their children.

The college curriculum is laid down on a plan that will not overwork pupils; but in order to maintain a good standing in any grade it will require application, industry, and study. Idle boys, indifferent to their recitations, will not be tolerated, but excused from the school. Irregular attendance or absence, unless caused by sickness, cannot be permitted. The object of the school is to make students, to teach children how to apply themselves, that they may become scholars, and that their conduct may be unexceptional. Too many are of the opinion that school work tends to weaken the constitution of children; the effect is quite to the contrary; at least nine out of every ten whose parents are able to give a good education at private schools will be benefited by strict school discipline. We do not mean overwork—but work. It refines the mind and strengthens the body. Nothing is so dangerous as idleness, and parents who do not wish their children to study or to come under the Rules and Regulations had better not send them.

Lectures.

A course of ten lectures will be delivered in the College Hall upon various subjects during the Fall and Winter. Proceeds for the benefit of the College Library. (Free to the pupils.)

ERRATA.

Page 6, fourteenth line from top, *Prof. Lowe,* instead of *Lovoe.*

Page 44, fifth line from the bottom, *we have sold,* instead of *we sold have.*

Page 224, ninth line from bottom, *White,* instead of *Whits.*

Page 228, under the head of "Expenses," *Day Pupils* should read *Boarding Pupils.*

The following description of five varieties of Eucalyptus-trees should have been inserted on folio 38 :

Eucalyptus goniocalyx, F. v. Mueller.—From Cape Otway to the southern parts of New South Wales. A large tree, which should be included among those for new plantations. Its wood resembles, in many respects, that of E. globulus. For house-building, fence-rails, and similar purposes, it is extensively employed in those forest districts where it is abundant, and has proved itself a valuable timber.

Eucalyptus hemiphloia, F. v. Mueller.—New South Wales and South Queensland. To be regarded as a timber-tree of great excellence, on the authority of the Rev. Dr. Woolls. It is famous for the hardness and toughness of its timber, which is used for shafts, spokes, plow-beams, and similar utensils.

Eucalyptus Leucoxylon, F. v. Mueller.—The ordinary iron-bark tree of Victoria and some parts of South Australia and New South Wales. As the supply of its very durable timber is falling short, and as it is for some purposes superior to that of almost any other Eucalypt, the regular culture of this tree over wide areas should be fostered, especially as it can be raised on stony ridges not readily available for ordinary husbandry. The wood is sometimes pale, or in other localities rather dark. The tree is generally restricted to the lower Silurian sandstone and slate formation, with iron-stone and quartz. It is rich in Kino. E. sideroxylon is a synonym.

Eucalyptus maculata, Hooker. — A spotted Gum-tree of New South Wales and South Queensland. A lofty tree, the wood of which is employed in ship-building, wheelwrights' and coopers' work. The heart-wood as strong as that of British Oak (Rev. Dr. Woolls).

Eucalyptus obliqua, L'Heritier.* — The ordinary stringy-bark tree, attaining gigantic dimensions. The most extensively-distributed and most gregarious of all Eucalypts, from Spencer's Gulf to the southern parts of New South Wales, and in several varieties designated by splitters and other wood-workers by different names; most extensively used for cheap fencing-rails, palings, shingles, and any other rough wood-work, not to be sunk under ground nor requiring great strength or elasticity. The bulk of wood obtained from this tree in very poor soil is perhaps larger than that of any other kind, and thus this species can be included even here, where it is naturally common and easily redisseminated, among the trees for new forest plantations in barren, woodless tracts of our own country, to yield readily and early a supply of cheap and easily fissile wood.

TEMPERATURE OF AIR IN SHADE FOR THE LAST FOURTEEN YEARS.

From the Observatory Records at Melbourne.

	HIGHEST.	LOWEST.	MEAN.
At Melbourne	111·2	27 0	57·6
At Sandhurst	117·4	27·5	59·0
At Ballarat	109·0	22·0	53.2
At Portland	108·0	30 0	61·5
At Port Albert	......	.....	56.5

RAINFALL AT MELBOURNE.

	INCH.		INCH.		INCH.
In 1857	28·90	In 1862	22·08	In 1867	25·79
In 1858	26·02	In 1863	36·43	In 1868	18·27
In 1859	21·80	In 1864	27·40	In 1869	24·59
In 1860	25·40	In 1865	15·94	In 1870	33·75
In 1861	29·15	In 1866	22·41	In 1871	30·17

TEM. OF AIR IN SHADE AT TWOFOLD BAY, 1871.

(Corresponding to the lowlands of East Gipps Land.)

From the Observatory Records of Sydney.

	MEAN.	M. MAX.	M. MIN.	E. MAX.	E. MIN.	R'FALL.
January	68·1	75·0	61·2	....	....	4·570
February	67·6	72·9	62·3	....	....	12·350
March	64·0	70·4	57·7	....	....	1·500
April	61·5	68·4	54·5	....	...	2·540
May	59·4	64·6	54·2	....	....	12·000
June	53·5	59·9	47·1	....	....	5·640
July	52·7	60·3	45·0	72·0	39·1	0·790
August	52 8	60·8	44·7	68·0	41·1	0·690
September	56·7	63·8	49·5	73·0	44·1	1·530
October	58·1	65·9	50·2	76·0	42·1	8·270
November	63·4	71·6	55 2	81·0	47·1	2·390
December	70·4	79·7	61·1	106·0	54·1	1·470

60·7° mean annual temperature. 53·740 inches rainfall for the year.

TEM. OF AIR IN SHADE AT TWOFOLD BAY, 1872.

From the Magistrate's Office at Eden.

	MAX.	MIN.	R'FALL.
	Deg.	Deg.	Inches.
January	88·0	61·0	3·15
February	83·0	63·0	1·15
March	81·0	58·0	1·92
April	62·0	55·0	1·03
May	62·0	47·0	1·08

www.ingramcontent.com/pod-product-compliance
Lightning Source LLC
LaVergne TN
LVHW050515100826
845148LV00002B/344

* 9 7 8 1 4 2 5 5 2 1 4 1 7 *